Taking Up Your Role

How to Shift Between Life and Work Without Losing Yourself

Anna-Lena Sundlin
& Paul Sundlin

Taking Up Your Role

ISBN 978-0-9858721-3-7

© 2014 Anna-Lena Sundlin and Paul Sundlin

All rights reserved. No part of this book may be reproduced or utilized in any form or by any means, electronic or mechanical, including photocopying, recording, or by any information storage and retrieval system, without written permission from the authors or the publisher.

Catalyst Communications Press
175 Richdale Avenue, Suite 106
Cambridge, MA 02140
Orders & customer service: 800.600.1522
Online orders: http://catalystpress.bigcartel.com

Originally published in Sweden under the title *Ta din roll på jobbet!* by Liber AB
Swedish edition copyright © 2012 Anna-Lena Sundlin, Paul Sundlin, and Liber AB

Translators: Helena Sjöstedt-Ware and Amy Yeager
Editors, English edition: Amy Yeager and Ben Benjamin
Editor, Swedish edition: Charlotte Rudenstam
Cover illustration: Jamel Akib
Cover concept: Felix Rust
Cover design: Amy Yeager and Erica Schultz
Illustrations: Jonny Hallberg
Typesetting: Erica Schultz

CONTENTS

Foreword 9
Foreword to the English Edition 11
Preface 13
Introduction 15

Chapter 1. Contexts and roles in our daily lives 19
    Person and situation 19
    The concept of roles 21
    Habitual roles 22
    Professions in transition 23
    Taking up a functional role 24
    Context – goal – role 24

Chapter 2. Separating the role from the person 27
    When the person merges with the job 27
    Boundaries 28
    When boundaries get blurred 29
    The value of mental boundaries 30
    The permeability of boundaries 30
    What's involved in a professional role? 31
    The consequences of unclear roles 33

Chapter 3. Moving stones versus building a cathedral 35
    Setting visible and understandable goals 35
    Defining a clear task 36
    A sense of coherence 37

CONTENTS

Chapter 4. Living human systems 39
Basic principles of systems thinking 40
Clear boundaries 40
Permeability—peepholes to the outside 42
Common goals 44
The organization—a Russian doll................................45

Chapter 5. The importance of having a functioning filter ..49
External reminders 49
Internal work..51
Picturing the filter 51
Requirements for a functioning filter 53
Personal responsibility...54
When you slip out of your role....................................55

Chapter 6. What's the point of having a boss?..............59
Leadership and the manager's role 59
The manager as boundary straddler..............................61
Functional hierarchy...62
The manager's role in the hierarchy..............................63
Considerations for the employee.................................64
The employee/manager relationship 65

Chapter 7. Meetings, meetings, and more meetings 67
Why we need meetings...67
Saying the right thing in the wrong context 68
Communication and plumbing 71
Meetings: function-structure-person 72
Small action—great effect 74

Chapter 8. Looking through the lens of group development..........77
An integrated model of group development 77
Stage 1: Security and belonging 79
Stage 2: Opposition and conflict........80
Stage 3: Trust and structure 81
Stage 4: Work and productivity........82
Not always a linear progression 82
The employee's role as a group member........83
A fly on the wall 83

Chapter 9. Thought as a tool 87
Past, present, and future 87
Facts and interpretations 89
Here and now 90
A model for understanding our thought patterns 90
Interpretations of the past: War stories and nostalgia........91
Interpretations of the future: Fears and fantasies 92
Interpretations of the present: Mind-reading 93
Learning from the past 94
Planning for the future 94
Being present 95
Applying the model to your workplace 96

Chapter 10. Hanging in for the long haul 99
Contextual factors that help us take up our role........99
What can we do ourselves? 100
Don't reinvent the wheel........100

References........103

FOREWORD

You hold in your hand an instruction manual for a tool called *role*. Like all good tools, it makes work easier, more efficient, and above all, more fun. Many tools are accompanied by instruction manuals that are complicated and hard to read. This book is different in that respect. It is easy to read and logically organized. Once you understand the concepts, they will make perfect sense to you. You will be able to put the manual aside and take up your role at work, maybe in a new and more authentic and functional way.

How can one word, one concept, be a tool? Think about building a house. The process requires complicated calculations of strength and physical forces. If we did not have access to such abstract concepts, it would be difficult to build houses that are safe to live in. The same is true of working relationships and social contexts. It is important that we understand what we're doing and why one course of action moves us forward, while another may lead to frustration and confusion.

The word *role* is a mundane term that has many connotations. Probably the most common association is with acting. As a result, it may seem as though taking on a role has something to do with putting on an act. This is in stark contrast to an ideal that many of us share—namely, to be yourself and not try to be somebody you're not.

The reality is that even in acting, there is no contradiction between staying in a role and staying true to yourself. An actor is his own instrument. Would it be possible to play somebody else on stage without at the same time being yourself? Think about some of the great movie actors. Whenever you see them in a film, you can probably recognize them by their tone of voice or other distinguishing characteristics. They are themselves at the same time as they are playing a role. You could say that they've found a sounding board within themselves for the character (or role) that they're portraying. The concept of role that is described in this book is

FOREWORD

based on exactly this principle—that you need to find the part of yourself that corresponds to your task within the organization. In this way, you can be yourself at the same time as you take up your role.

In a work context, a role is often described as a position or a task that we are expected to perform. We talk about the different expectations we have of different roles, such as what a teacher, nurse, musician, or manager is expected to do, and often also how that person is expected to behave. You could say that roles lend a structure to the work.

This structure always involves a certain amount of hierarchy. We have to accept that hierarchies are unavoidable in our social system. Provided that they are based on sound values such as fairness, respect, and predictability, they build trust and security. The challenge is to develop hierarchies that are stable enough to provide order and clarity, but not so rigid that they lead to bureaucracy or isolated silos. Like all living systems, organizations are constantly changing and evolving. To serve our organizations well, our role structures must be able to change and evolve as well.

In this book, the authors clarify all of these concepts and describe in an easily accessible manner the dynamic process involved in adopting a role. Their underlying theory of roles has its roots in systems theory. One of the prominent figures in this school of thought, Kurt Lewin, once said that there is nothing so practical as a good theory. As you continue reading, you'll see how true that is. Enjoy!

Lund, September 2011
Christer Sandahl
Professor of Social and Behavioural Sciences
Karolinska Institutet, Stockholm, Sweden

FOREWORD TO THE ENGLISH EDITION

We are very pleased to be asked to write the foreword for Anna-Lena and Paul's new book. Anna-Lena is a dear friend, colleague and valued systems-centered (SCT) trainee for many years now and Paul too, though for not quite so long. We congratulate them for this easy-to-read book that will be of value to their clients and others interested in working with the idea of role in organizations (and as they note, "role in everyday life").

Anna-Lena and Paul present their adaptations of theories and models that have influenced their practice as psychologists and organizational consultants. We are gratified to see how the influence of SCT infuses much of their book as they have adapted the theory of living human systems and its systems-centered practice (SCT) (Agazarian, 1997; Gantt, S.P. & Agazarian, Y.M. (Eds.), 2006).

They have also particularly emphasized the importance of the concept of 'role.' In our systems-centered work, "Role" is also an important construct, and has specific significance in the SCT model of "role, goal and context."

Anna-Lena and Paul have successfully adapted SCT's model of Role, Goal and Context as their guiding tool for understanding and viewing roles in one's daily life. They illustrate their use of this tool with pictures and examples and exercises that the reader can use themselves. Their examples are especially useful in giving practical tips and demonstrating how they have adapted SCT theory in their practice. They emphasize that taking up one's role is not suppressing one's feelings or values.

In SCT, defining a role as a system has enabled us to understand in our own practice how, on the one hand, self-centeredness reflects a closed-boundaried role supporting survival, and on the other hand, it maintains survival at the expense of system development. The cost is that it restricts the person in relating freely as a member to their contexts, be it at work or at home or even with oneself. This major focus in SCT has revolutionized our work with clients and organizations, enabling us to support the person relating to the goals of their context. We are glad that Anna-Lena and Paul have adapted SCT in their approach and are making it available to a new population.

Yvonne Agazarian
Founder, Systems-Centered Training & Research Institute

Susan Gantt
Director, Systems-Centered Training & Research Institute

PREFACE

In writing this book, we set out to explain the concept of roles in an easily accessible and reader-friendly way, translating complex ideas from academic and theoretical contexts into language that any layperson could understand. As part of our effort to enhance the readability and flow of the text, we decided not to use formal citations. However, we do want to be clear about where these ideas originated. What follows is a brief summary of the many individuals and theoretical systems that have influenced us.

Our first encounter with systems theory and the concept of "role" was in the 1980s, through our work in clinical psychology. We were influenced by systemic family therapy (as practiced by the Milan school and others), which emphasized the need to understand each individual as existing within a larger context. Within this approach, the concept of habitual and dysfunctional roles was of central importance. In working with substance abuse, we came across similar ideas in models for transactional analysis and relapse prevention. Another important source of inspiration for us was Aaron Antonovsky's concept of "a sense of coherence," with his exploration of the universal human need to find meaning and to see ourselves in a larger context.

When we left clinical work in the 1990s and moved into the field of organizational psychology, we encountered new perspectives on the concept of roles, including an emphasis on the importance of clear goals for the development of functional roles. We were influenced by Poul Moxnes' work on how dysfunctional roles develop in the workplace, as well as Meredith Belbin's work on team roles, Elliott Jaques' thoughts on the requirements for a functional role-taking in an organizational hierarchy, Peter Lang's concept of systemic management, and Bruce Reed's theory and practice with role analysis.

In the late 1990s, Anna-Lena came into contact with Yvonne Agazarian and her theory of living human systems, and got involved in her systems-centered training (SCT). She was impressed by the comprehensiveness of this work—the way it integrated the concepts of role, goal, and context in systems at all levels, from individual people to large organizations. She introduced Paul, who became equally interested. Since then, Yvonne Agazarian's theory and SCT have had a great influence on our work and how we think about roles. In addition to forming the basis for our explanation of living human systems (Chapter 4) and model for understanding thought patterns (Chapter 9), these frameworks help to inform all of the discussions of roles, goals, and contexts in this book.

Another important influence in recent years has been Susan Wheelan's integrated theory of group development, which we have found to be an invaluable tool when working with groups and helping people take up functional roles. We've devoted a full chapter (Chapter 8) to the topic of group development, discussing how Wheelan's model applies to teams in an organizational context.

The ideas in this book are the result of all of our previous influences and experiences, with a major emphasis on adapting Yvonne Agazarian's work on role, goal, and context to everyday life at the workplace. We are delighted that Yvonne Agazarian and Susan Gantt (Director of the Systems-Centered Training and Research Institute) agreed to write the foreword to the English edition of our book.

INTRODUCTION

We humans have an inner compass that we use to find a meaningful direction in life. We possess a healthy degree of concern for ourselves and our own personal development, while also being willing to cooperate and develop together with others.

At the same time, we all have a basic tendency to be self-centered. We can easily create difficulties in our lives by getting too wrapped up in ourselves and losing sight of the bigger picture, leading to frustration, hurt feelings, and conflict.

This tendency can be particularly problematic for us at work. We lose sight of the purpose and goals of the tasks at hand and make decisions based on our own personal agenda. We take proposals for change as personal criticism and find it hard to contribute in a constructive way when things don't turn out exactly as we would have liked.

In our work as psychologists and organizational consultants, it has become increasingly clear that many workplace difficulties can be eliminated or drastically reduced if both managers and employees become less self-focused. This requires building understanding and actively working together with close colleagues to change attitudes in the workplace and structure the tasks in such a way that each individual can reach their full potential in their professional role.

In our view, the workplace is not a forum for general self-realization; rather, it is a distinct sphere of life where those parts of ourselves that are useful for the organization as a whole can grow and develop.

Our experience shows that when managers and employees receive tools and techniques to clarify their roles, positive changes follow. Their responsibilities, boundaries, rights, and obligations become much clearer, and personal conflicts, stress, and feelings of insecurity start to diminish.

INTRODUCTION

Of course, there are factors in the outside world that affect an organization's ability to change and survive. But those things that are beyond our control are no reason to avoid making positive changes in our immediate working environment. There are always areas that can be improved, and those are what we will be focusing on in the following pages.

This book is intended for anyone who feels inspired to improve their ability to take up their professional role and to collaborate with others to reach common goals. You can use it both as a starting point for your own reflections and as a source of concrete guidance at work.

Taking Up Your Role

CHAPTER 1
Contexts and roles in our daily lives

As we begin to explore what professional roles are and how they may need to be adjusted, it helps to place the idea in a larger social and psychological context. In our lives, we play many different roles, and we may go back and forth between these roles many times in a single day, depending on the situation. At work, you may be a salesperson, doctor, or car mechanic, but you may also be a passenger on a bus or subway, as well as a parent, musician, or soccer coach. The list of these roles could go on and on.

The challenge we face is to find a balance between the different roles we play in our lives so that there is room for important aspects of ourselves to come forward in appropriate, useful ways.

Person and situation

Our personality is made up of different characteristics, thoughts, feelings, and patterns of behavior that are typical for every individual and that make us different from other people. In addition, we all have memories and ideas about the past that affect the way we look at reality, as well as specific knowledge, experience, and values that shape our way of being.

Yet we never express our entire personality—with all of its resources and limitations—at the same time. We display different versions of ourselves depending on how we interpret different contexts, including what we think is required or expected and

CHAPTER 1

what we think is the most normal or customary behavior. We use some characteristics and abilities, while leaving out other aspects of ourselves that we intuitively or rationally realize do not fit the situation.

For instance, at the playground, a father may allow his playful side to come forward, laughing and goofing around with his child who wants to be pushed higher and higher on the swing or be wrestled to the ground. Later that day, waiting in line at the bank, it's unlikely that he'd express that same playful side and start doing a jig with the other customers.

Stubbornness is another example. When we need help troubleshooting a computer problem, it's good to work with someone who never gives up (and who also knows a lot about computers). But when we're playing beach volleyball on a beautiful summer evening and there is a disagreement about the rules, the same type of stubbornness could ruin the friendly atmosphere.

Most of us have the ability to understand which aspects of our personality we need to use based on the situation and the context. And most of the time, there is no need to work out a plan or carefully consider in advance how we should act. When we're growing up, we learn a lot about how to behave in various situations. This is why hardly anybody needs coaching on how to act when they go shopping, attend a concert, or visit the doctor.

However, we often do need help knowing how to act when we start a new job or move to another country with a different culture; our standard behavioral patterns don't always work in the new context.

When we don't understand how to behave in a certain situation, or don't know which parts of our personality need to come to the fore, things can get complicated.

> **A married couple** visits a therapist to try to work through the problems in their relationship. The woman is in tears as she talks about how they don't communicate any more. The man remains silent. When the therapist invites him to speak, his comment relates not to

his marriage but to his great interest in literature: he asks the therapist if she has read all the books on the shelves in the room. The wife shakes her head.

While an interest in literature can hardly be seen as inappropriate or destructive on its own, in this context—and bearing in mind the purpose of the meeting—his question can be seen as intentionally provocative.

The implied or explicit goal of a meeting or shared activity largely determines how we assess and value each other's behavior and patterns of communication. Behavior that is seen as correct and proper in one context may be viewed as clumsy, unwise, or irresponsible in another.

The concept of roles

We "take up our role" when our thoughts, feelings, behaviors, and patterns of communicating are appropriate to the context in which we find ourselves. Our focus and resources are directed toward the goal at hand, which is the reason for the very existence of the context.

This does not mean we need to pretend or misrepresent ourselves to the people around us. Nor do we need to set aside everything personal and important to us, turning off our feelings or suppressing our values.

An art director needs to use her organizational and planning skills when attending a project meeting at work. Her doubts as to whether this job actually satisfies her creative desires have nothing to do with the agenda of the meeting. Nor does her worry about her teenage daughter falling in love with the most complicated boy in her class. It's best for her not to allow these concerns to color her thought processes or her way of responding to the arguments or contributions of others. It's also important for her to resist being swayed by her personal positive or negative feelings toward the colleagues in the room with her.

CHAPTER 1

> **A soccer forward** is expected to primarily stay in the penalty area of the other team, so that she can fulfill her main function: scoring goals. When she kicks the ball into the goal, this contributes to her team's overall objective: to win the game. If the forward spends too much time in defense and not enough time attacking, she does not step into the role or fulfill the function that the context requires.

It may seem obvious that when we're at work, we should adapt to the demands of the situation and the function we're expected to perform. Yet there are many organizations in which the working climate is shaped by the personal needs of individuals and the inability of various groups to work together due to personal conflicts.

In addition, many organizations fail to make it sufficiently clear to their managers and employees what is expected of them and what their overall task and goals are. This is like telling somebody to get out onto a soccer field to kick the ball, but failing to explain why or in which direction.

Habitual roles

A typical example of a *habitual role* is the pattern of behavior that we tend to develop as an older or younger sibling. The positions we hold early in life can have a strong influence on the way we behave and relate to the people around us.

You may notice these sorts of roles in connection with a family reunion: the 52-year-old sister takes the lead and arranges things, while her 45-year-old younger brother cruises around trying to create a nice atmosphere. In their professional lives, the older sister may take on too much work, while her little brother finds a way to take a back seat and get his colleagues to handle projects that should probably be his responsibility.

People may also be heavily influenced by stereotypical gender roles. A man who in a previous relationship used to perform classically male tasks, and never did any housework, will be somewhat confused—and possibly hurt or irritated—if his new partner says she expects him to do the vacuuming every other Friday. A woman who has always played the role of quiet and unassuming female may get a sinking feeling in her gut if a new colleague asks for her opinion and expects a genuine response.

Other types of habitual roles include the class clown who even as an adult feels responsible for lightening the mood in tense situations, and "mother's little helper" who always feels compelled to offer assistance when her coworkers have a problem.

It's not necessarily wrong to play habitual roles, provided that those roles are functional in the current situation or relationship. But many habitual roles have an expiration date. They stem from an earlier context that no longer exists. When we use attitudes and behaviors that we feel safe with in a context where they do not fit, the result is friction and interpersonal difficulties.

Professions in transition

To thrive in today's society, we need a high degree of flexibility and a willingness to let go of old, familiar roles. Certain professions have undergone such major changes that the tasks, methods, and responsibilities involved look radically different today compared to 10 or 20 years ago. There are advertising illustrators who never touch a pencil and instead sit at a computer all day, and there are commercial pilots who rarely fly manually and spend most of their time making sure that the autopilot does its job.

There are many examples of previously familiar, safe professional roles and competencies that are no longer useful and need to be further developed, supplemented, or even completely eliminated. The latter may sound cruel, but the past bears witness to numerous jobs that no longer exist or are peripheral in the greater scheme of things. Where can you find people to repair typewriters today? Can anyone recommend a good milliner?

Taking up a functional role

Organizations and associations have certain overall purposes, as well as more specific goals. The individuals involved need to be clear about these, and about what their roles are and what functions they're expected to perform. Soccer team scrimmages, onboarding for new hires, and management trainings are all examples of activities that prepare people to take on a functional role in different contexts.

It's important to be able to accept and fulfill a new, functional role instead of staying in an old, comfortable role or playing a different role that we'd personally prefer to play. It is equally important to be ready for that role to shift, to be willing to understand when our established ways of working or outlook on life need to change. What used to be practical and effective may not be any more. And we don't have to take that personally.

The parent of a young child must try to keep up when the little angel who used to line up his stuffed animals in a neat row suddenly turns into an irresponsible, untidy creature whose messiness requires a very different type of parenting. An engineer who stubbornly clings to old technologies will be left behind and lose his status as an expert. And an adult student who comes into the classroom expecting a traditional lecture format, and therefore avoids group discussions and independent learning, will have difficulty succeeding academically.

Context – goal – role

We live in a society that is rapidly changing, in both the professional and the personal sphere. In addition, as we've been discussing here, we are constantly switching between different roles. Therefore, it is important to define which context we are in, what the goal is, and what role we are expected to play or want to play. The model on the following page may be used as an analytical tool to help us do this.

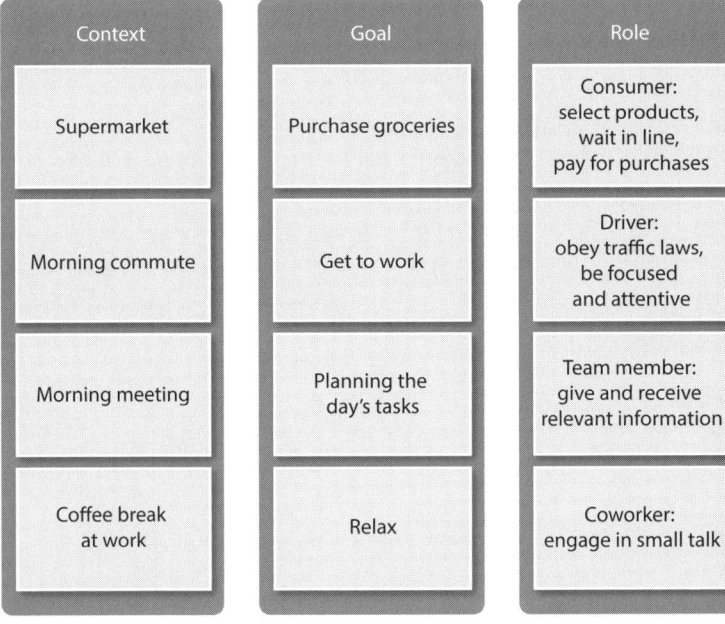

EXERCISE

The examples above show how to use the model. Copy it and fill it in with situations from your own daily life:

- Enter different contexts in the column on the left.
- Identify what the goal is for each context and enter this in the middle column.
- Consider how you can best contribute to the given context in order to reach the goal. Can you find an appropriate term for the role you play? Enter this term in the right-hand column.

The point of this exercise is to make you more aware of the various roles you play in a day. It also gives you an opportunity to discover whether you are unclear about the goal of different contexts or about how you can make a valuable contribution.

CHAPTER 1

The exercise is particularly useful in contexts where you need to work together with others—for example, in discussing how to increase participation at PTA meetings, or agreeing on how ambitious you want your amateur theater production to be.

Perhaps its most useful purpose is to clarify certain aspects of your job, either for you alone or for your team as a whole. Which contexts do you find yourself in during the workday? Do you and your colleagues agree on the purpose of different meetings and tasks? Do you agree on what your goals are and what you need to do in order to achieve them?

CHAPTER 2

Separating the role from the person

Separating the role from the person may at first seem like an artificial and overly analytical task. However, we can benefit greatly from this type of thinking. It is important to differentiate between our self as a whole and the version of ourselves that we need to embody at work. This helps to protect us from losing sight of the overall purpose of the work and from taking things too personally.

One area where the importance of the role/person distinction is particularly clear is in volunteering, where we invest a lot of our personal time managing the activities of our favorite club or association. When we put our heart and soul into these efforts, we may find it hard to separate our own interests from those of the larger organization. If people critique or raise objections to our work, we may feel unfairly treated, since we have sacrificed so much for the sake of the "cause." Unfortunately, similar problems are also quite common in our professional lives when the boundary between role and person gets blurred.

When the person merges with the job

Just as some people live for their hobbies, others live for their work. They identify so strongly with their profession that they allow it to overshadow virtually everything else in their lives. Their emotional and intellectual engagement in their job extends far beyond regular business hours and performance reviews.

In particular, individuals in creative professions such as writers, musicians, and sculptors can easily lose a sense of the boundaries between themselves and their life's work. Other examples include researchers who spend many hours each day in a laboratory and self-employed businesspeople who personify an optimistic, entrepreneurial spirit. It's not uncommon for these types of professions to be romanticized by the general public. There is something attractive about people who become totally absorbed and passionate about one thing.

People who focus so fully on their job usually love it and can't imagine doing anything else. Some people consciously choose to avoid starting a family or engaging in any other activities that would take their energy away from what they want to spend their lives doing. Even if they agree to a certain extent that it's important to distinguish between their professional role and their private life, many tend to resist separating the two; they worry that their professional role will be too constricting, limiting their freedom to "just be themselves." For these individuals, the self and the job have become one.

If we identify too strongly with our professional role and skills, we risk losing a healthy distance from our work. Criticism of our efforts may feel like an affront to our dignity. When external conditions require our professional role to change, we may feel insulted over something that is not at all directed toward us personally.

Boundaries

There are of course people who love their job and also lead a fulfilling life outside of their professional role—people who distinguish between who they are at work and who they are in their living room. To most of us, this separation seems like intuitive common sense, and we try to live accordingly. Some of us intentionally choose hobbies that are as different as possible from our jobs. Somebody with an emotionally draining job in which they're constantly interacting with other people may have a hobby constructing model boats. People who spend all day in a position of leadership may find it relaxing to sing in a choir and be led by a director.

No matter how much we enjoy our professional role, it's helpful to have an area of our lives where there is room for other things: relaxing, developing different sides of ourselves, or simply being left alone to perform the mundane tasks involved in the other roles we have. We feel instinctively that something is wrong when we keep waking up in the middle of the night worrying about problems at work.

When boundaries get blurred

But reality does not always meet our needs for mental boundaries. Sometimes different roles and areas of our lives merge into each other, making it hard to separate out our thoughts, feelings, and behaviors:

- **A middle school teacher** who is struggling with a rowdy eighth grade class has equally boisterous teenagers at home.
- **A manager of a nursing home** makes daily visits to her elderly mother, who is suffering from dementia.
- **A psychotherapist** needs therapy himself after a close relative passes away.

Under such circumstances, it's easy to go astray:

- **The middle school teacher** overreacts to an irreverent student because her son behaved badly at breakfast.
- **The manager of a nursing home** becomes so emotionally affected by the tears of a resident's relative that she loses her ability to listen attentively.
- **The psychotherapist** starts making mental comparisons between his patient's problems and his own inner turmoil.

The value of mental boundaries

Having a conceptual framework of the differences between our professional and personal roles gives us a foundation to rely on when changes at work or at home make life uncertain and unpredictable.

The following breakdown can help in creating a mental separation between our professional role and our personality as a whole:

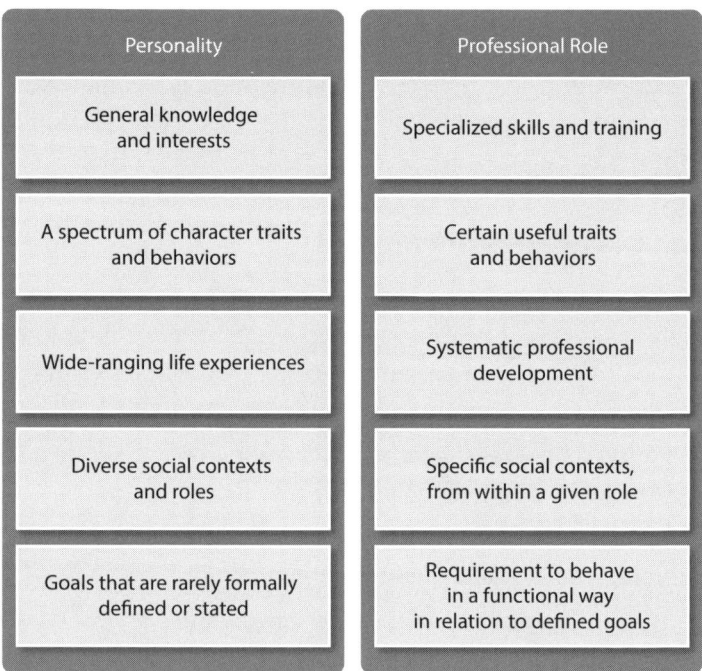

The permeability of boundaries

The separation between our personality and professional role can seem a bit rigid—suggesting that our life experiences evolve separately from what happens at work, or that the development we experience in the course of our career leaves no traces in our personality. This is obviously not the case.

On the contrary, a person's career can have a great positive influence on their overall level of maturity. Young people working in the helping professions may experience situations that have a crucial impact on their compassion toward others and their general outlook on life. Managers who struggle with difficult decisions and must live with the long-term consequences learn a lot about how people act and react in stressful circumstances.

In addition, many people can attest that their personal experiences have improved their job performance. After a year of maternity leave, a kindergarten teacher returns to work with a better perspective on what it means to be a parent, which in turn leads to a wiser and more patient attitude toward the parents of her students. After overcoming significant shyness in his private life, an economist starts to feel more confident presenting forecasts and budget follow-ups to the management team.

In other words, there is an interaction between the lessons we learn on the job and what we experience in our private lives.

What's involved in a professional role?

A professional role can be roughly divided into two areas, both requiring sufficient competence. The first of those is the obvious one: performing the concrete, practical duties that make up the job. A surgeon must be able to perform operations, putting into practice all of her surgical skill and knowledge about the human body. A janitor must be able to use a variety of different cleaning supplies to keep a building clean and tidy. A journalist must be able to use language to present information in an organized and coherent way.

Most professions require some form of basic training and continuing education. Often there is documentation to prove that we have obtained a certain level of professional skill: diplomas, certificates, professional licenses, and so forth. It is becoming increasingly clear that we need to keep ourselves up-to-date in our skills so as not to fall behind in our field.

The second component of the professional role is more elusive and intangible. It has to do with working well together with other people, both within one's team and outside it—being able to communicate and listen to others with sensitivity and respect. The surgeon needs to create a trusting relationship with her patient. The janitor needs to effectively discuss the distribution of work with his colleagues. And the journalist needs to actively participate in various editorial meetings.

To an ever-increasing degree, the modern workplace requires cooperation between colleagues and outside professionals, which means that we need to become more aware that we form part of a greater context. This includes the ability to compromise, to respect the values and opinions of other people, and to reflect on our own behavior and correct it if necessary.

The two aspects of the professional role can be summed up as follows:

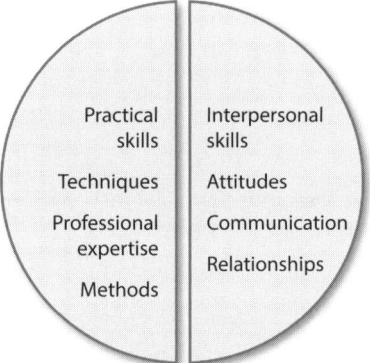

> **EXERCISE**
>
> With your own professional role in mind, fill in the two halves of the circle with elements that are useful in each area. Then figure out what definitely does not belong and place these elements outside the circle. In this way, you can clarify the contents and boundaries of your role. This model can also serve as a road map for managers and employees during a performance review or as a starting point for discussing roles and functions with colleagues.

The consequences of unclear roles

If a person's employer fails to convey to them what is included in each half of the circle, their role becomes very fuzzy. Frequently, of course, the main practical aspects of the job are clear enough: drive the bus from point A to point B, sit at the checkout counter and accept people's payments, teach the students history, and so forth. However, in many workplaces, there is little clarity about which attitudes and behaviors are desirable. This opens the way for individuals to act based on their own personal values rather than the mission and values of the organization.

Obviously, it's important to have our values respected in different contexts, but in a workplace we need to join together and operate in accordance with the purpose of the work, with a focus on achieving the goals of that work. If the management fails to explain the common purpose, we go with what we know—namely, ourselves—and make do with that. When several people within a work group base their professional actions on themselves, this often leads to friction and a lack of cooperation. Such problems are frequently explained by describing the individuals involved as "difficult," or suffering from poor personal chemistry, but in reality they are a consequence of a lack of clarity and consensus on the direction of the work.

An inefficient staff is often a symptom of unclear roles and unclear direction. If there are no clear indications as to *what* needs to be done and *why,* and what limits there are on our freedom to structure the work in our own way, our professional role necessarily becomes ambiguous for us and the people around us.

Confusion regarding roles at work can cause stress and frustration among employees. Other consequences include disorganized meetings that lack a clear order of priorities, personal conflicts that flare up in work contexts where they don't belong, and concerns about what one's colleagues or managers are *actually* doing.

CHAPTER 3
Moving stones versus building a cathedral

Participating in a group—whether it's a running club, a condo association board, or an executive team—becomes rather boring and pointless if the purpose of the group's activities is not clear. We need to understand the big picture of why we're working together. Without a purpose or more far-reaching vision, many groups lose their momentum, and participants have difficulty staying interested and engaged.

> A person sees two men carrying stones. She asks the first one what he is doing and he says with a sigh:
>
> *I am moving stones.*
>
> She asks the other one the same question, and he replies:
>
> *I am building a cathedral.*

Setting visible and understandable goals

Most organizations have clear purposes and goals at an overall, general level. The difficulties arise in translating those abstract, high-level objectives into concrete, understandable goals for the departments, teams, and individuals that do the day-to-day work of the organization. What the management sees as obvious concerns are often perceived by the employees as vague, ambiguous ideals.

In addition, it's easy to underestimate how long it takes to flesh out different formulations of goals, so that they become useful tools for shaping people's roles and working methods. Yet this process is of vital importance if a workplace is to be able to function as it's intended to. It is in the everyday actions of all the people performing various tasks that the purpose and goals of the organization are realized.

If a doctor or therapist kept yawning or looking at their watch while we were sitting there telling them about our problems, we'd have no trouble recognizing that their behavior was not in keeping with their role. And if a waiter openly scoffed at our choice of wine for dinner, we'd be convinced that there was something very wrong with the restaurant's hiring process. However, the discrepancies between how somebody behaves in their role and what is actually expected in relation to the overall goal are rarely so obvious—which is exactly why they are so important to discover and remedy.

If one of the core values of a certain hospital is *respect,* how can this respect be expressed through one's role within the pharmacy, the IT department, or the janitorial staff?

If a company wishes to clarify and work toward meeting their environmental targets, will that mean any specific change in how the switchboard operators perform their task, or will it affect only the sales and marketing departments?

Visible, understandable goals at all levels of an organization simplify the process of shaping the duties and responsibilities of working groups and individuals.

Defining a clear task

Since many workplaces allow groups and individuals a relatively high degree of freedom in how they plan and carry out their tasks, it's important that each task be clearly spelled out and in line with the purpose and the goals of the organization.

The reason why we're given some leeway to shape our own roles is that this allows us to do a better job. As a result, job satisfaction increases, and this in turn directly and indirectly contributes to success, profit, optimal service, or whatever else is being strived for.

But there is also a risk of forgetting why we are being paid; personal ingenuity can become an end in itself, and the flexible routines we've created for ourselves may become so important to us that we lose sight of our original task.

The importance of clear agreements and tasks is generally most obvious to us in situations where we hire somebody to do a specific job. In this case, the connection between task, completed work, and paid compensation is very clear.

When we go to a hair salon, we agree on the haircut we want. We probably would not be willing to pay if the stylist decided to stop in the middle of the haircut or insisted that we let him dye our hair with what we see as a catastrophic mix of colors.

Nobody would hire a carpenter and instruct him to "come and do a bit of carpentry," and then happily pay for whatever he did. We would always give more specific instructions about what needs to be done, such as installing shelves in a particular closet. If the carpenter decided to put in new kitchen cabinets instead and expected us to be grateful, we would naturally protest.

Yet as clear as we are about roles when we hire someone else to perform a service, we often lack clarity about our own responsibilities in our daily lives at work. Instead, we work based on very general instructions and take it for granted that our salary will be paid just because we show up each day. It's easy to forget that our employment is a business agreement, just like the one with the carpenter or the hair stylist. We are employed to carry out a certain task, to fulfill a certain function in relation to the organization. In return for this, an agreed-upon compensation is paid. On the formal level, it's as simple as that.

A sense of coherence

Human beings are meaning seekers. In whatever we do, we want there to be a purpose, a direction, a feeling that we are acting on the basis of intelligent and purposeful motives. The purpose of a certain task need not be grand, the motive behind an activity need not be unique, but we feel good when we see that we are contributing to the realization of a vision or a positive end result.

In the workplace, a sense of a larger vision is essential for giving meaning to what we do and keeping us actively engaged and interested in the organization as a whole. Both managers and employees have a critical responsibility to maintain an ongoing dialogue about how this vision is to be kept alive.

CHAPTER 4

Living human systems

When we lose sight of the big picture, we miss out on an opportunity to infuse our work with a broader and deeper meaning. And yet, this approach comes very naturally to us. It's easy to get fixated on details, narrow the focus of our thinking, and base our actions on a very limited amount of information. As a result, we often fail to fully understand the problems we wish to solve, making it impossible to find effective solutions and make informed decisions. Instead of taking close-ups of reality, we need to work on taking a few steps back and studying it from a wider perspective.

> **A student** who is restless and unruly in the classroom often gets labeled as a problem child. It's easy to individualize the issue and see the child's behavior as a consequence of a difficult family situation or mental health disorder. We may be quick to get counselors, psychologists, or special education staff involved. This is not necessarily wrong. However, if we fail to also take into account the relationships between the students, the overall climate in the classroom, and any disruptive transitions that are occurring within the school, we reduce our chances of adequately understanding and addressing the situation.

In order to handle challenging situations successfully, we need to remember to take our eyes off the ground and consider the surrounding context. The same is true for taking up our role in a functional way. It can be useful to think in more abstract terms, looking at things from a systems perspective.

Systems thinking helps us to remember that nothing happens in a vacuum—that all people and events form part of a greater context.

When we realize this, we can also see that it's possible to navigate between different contexts more effectively. We get a clearer picture of what is expected of our own role in different situations, and can channel our information and behaviors in the right direction. In this way, we can conserve our energy and focus on what is important.

Systems theory is a broad and complex area that has been described by a variety of researchers and writers. The following argument is adapted from psychologist Yvonne Agazarian's theory of living human systems.

Basic principles of systems thinking

Individuals, groups, and organizations can all be viewed as living human systems. From that perspective, we can see that although these systems operate at different levels—from a single person to a large and complex institution—they share some common basic principles that govern their life and development. They are all inherently goal-oriented and capable of adapting to different contexts, and they all develop through the same essential process: taking in new and different information and integrating it with what is already known. In order to function properly, they all require clear boundaries, permeability, and common goals. The following sections explain these principles in greater detail.

Clear boundaries

A system can be depicted as a circle. The border of the circle symbolizes the boundary between what happens inside the system and what exists outside it, in the external environment.

The individual level

At the level of the individual, the inside of the system consists of all of our thoughts, feelings, knowledge, experiences, and personality traits.

The surrounding environment consists of the situation we're in and the people we're interacting with. The human body forms a tangible boundary that distinguishes the individual system from its surroundings, and normally, we have a fairly clear mental picture of how we are separated from the world around us. One exception is when we find ourselves in an emotionally intense relationship (for instance, when we've just fallen in love with someone or are bonding with a newborn baby); in this type of situation, our psychological boundaries can become blurred, so that we experience the line between "me" and "the other" as being much more fluid.

The group level

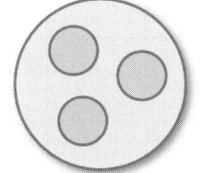

When an individual joins together with others in a working group, each person's role becomes a subsystem within the larger system. Within the group, there is an ongoing exchange between the subsystems; the members of the group do their work, relate to each other, and communicate among themselves. Ideally, those interactions are based upon the members' clearly delineated roles. In the area surrounding the working group are the other systems that the group serves and collaborates with: customers, clients, advisors, affiliates, partners, and so on.

The boundary of the group system is defined by the task that it has been given—the particular function it is expected to perform in the workplace. That boundary is not always clear and often requires more attention and clarification than one might think. One example of this is the problem of conflicting expectations regarding a human resources department. The boundaries of the department's various areas of responsibility may be unclear both to the HR staff themselves and to other people in the organization. For instance, when an employee is struggling with a mental health disorder, which HR division(s) should be involved? Benefits? Disability services? Legal? The work/life office or wellness center? When a manager seeks advice about taking disciplinary action, should the HR consultant be very specific and directive, or should they give more general guidance and let the manager figure out the details based on his or her management style?

The organizational level

The typical organization—comprised of several units and departments, with many groups working at different levels of a hierarchy and performing a wide range of functions—is a highly complex living human system with a large number of subsystems. Any hospital, corporation, university, or research facility encompasses many ongoing activities and interactions between individuals and within and between groups.

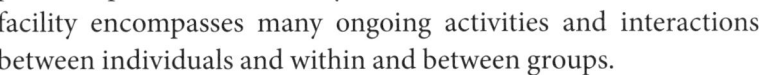

An organization's external environment consists of the society within which it operates; that includes customers, competitors, the state of the economy, any relevant legislation, and so forth. The system is defined by the organization's business idea, the details of what it is committed to producing and delivering. Without a clear and relevant definition of exactly what you're in the business of doing, it's difficult to stand out and stay competitive.

Permeability—peepholes to the outside

For a system to be functional, its boundaries must be clear. But clarity should not be confused with rigidity. A closed system loses touch with its surroundings and becomes stagnant. Living human systems have an amazing ability to self-correct, adapting to the changing demands of their environments. This can only happen when the boundary between the system and its surrounding context is permeable and open to new information.

The individual and the group

To function well in life and work, individuals must align their attitudes and behavior to the context they're in. If conditions change and we refuse to adapt, insisting on continuing to do what we've always done, we become closed systems that stand in the way of continued development. To contribute constructively in a working group, we also need to be able to listen to and take in other people's opinions and ideas, even if they differ from our own. This is a challenge for most of us, but absolutely necessary if we wish to benefit from the resources and skills of the entire system.

The same principle applies at the group level. The work done by a group needs to be in harmony with the larger context in which the group is functioning. For instance, the staff in a diner may have lots of fun together behind the kitchen door, but if that job satisfaction doesn't translate into good food served in a friendly manner, the group is out of harmony with its context. Likewise, if a team of youth counselors refuse to change their approach in response to the changing problems and needs of the young people they serve, that group becomes a dysfunctional, closed system.

Thus, both the individual and the group must have permeable boundaries to be able to navigate through their environment and work in a functional way. As individuals, we have a responsibility to stay current and open to new information. For a group, regular updates about what's happening outside the group may be necessary. It can be useful to charge a couple of people with the specific task of thinking strategically based on ongoing changes in the larger organizational context.

The organization and the outside world

Organizations, too, cannot afford to have closed boundaries. Such a large system requires a well-thought-out process for monitoring the external environment. If an organization has little or no knowledge of the changes that are currently taking place and are expected in the future, it will not survive. When companies rely too heavily on their own skills and products, not wanting to take in unpleasant information, they risk going bankrupt or being forced to cut back considerably on their business. Consider the automobile manufacturers that have failed to respond to customers' increased environmental awareness. They have missed the peepholes in the wall, or not bothered to look, and thus lost the ability to self-correct.

Common goals

All human systems have an inherent energy and are headed somewhere. The challenge is to guide the movement in an appropriate direction.

While choosing a direction may take a good deal of effort even for one individual planning their own life, the challenge becomes more obvious when a number of people are involved. Something as simple as a few colleagues going out for lunch may lead to considerable difficulties in working together. If things go badly, they may wind up on a long trek between different restaurants, becoming increasingly irritated as they discover that different individuals have different ideas about what type of lunch they're looking for; one of them wants a hearty meal, another person is on a strict low-carb diet, and a third doesn't like Asian food. In such situations, "going out for lunch" proves to be an insufficient goal, too vague to drive collaborative action.

Now just imagine how complicated it is to get an entire organization to navigate toward common goals. This is where various types of goal statements come into play. No matter what we call them—business plans, mission statements, balanced scorecards—they are all intended to help employees to move together toward a shared objective, to act and prioritize in a way that focuses their energy in the right direction. For this to happen, it is critical for the goal statements to be sufficiently concrete to be useful in daily life, and for everyone involved to be familiarized with them.

The organization—a Russian doll

The system levels in an organization form a contextual hierarchy that is layered like a Russian doll or an onion. The organization may, for example, contain the levels of division, department, team, and professional role. The task and direction of each level is determined by the larger context. Everyone needs to participate in order to fulfill the purpose of the organization and contribute to the overall goal.

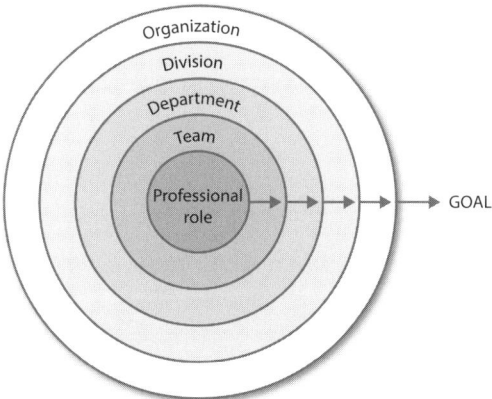

The starting point is the overall task that the organization performs and the overall goal it's working toward. Based on this, subtasks are created that get assigned to the next level, maybe to different divisions; together, these subtasks encompass everything that the organization needs to do. After this come the tasks of the departments within a particular division; each department performs one piece of the division's task, so that together they can achieve the division's overall goal. At the next level, the overall task of an individual department is distributed among teams. Finally, based on the task of the team as a whole, the professional roles within the team are defined. Every team member makes their individual contribution, and together they fulfill the overall purpose of the team.

CHAPTER 4

From the outside in

Business activities are shaped from the outside in, governed by the needs or demands in the wider world that comprise the organization's reason for being. This may sound obvious, but it's something that we as individual employees and managers easily forget and may periodically need to remind ourselves of. Awareness of that reality is essential in order to create and maintain the sense of purpose and broader context that we described in the previous chapter.

> **EXERCISE**
>
> Using the circle-and-arrow framework, create a concrete picture of the system levels involved in your own work. Follow the steps in the example below. Use documents such as business plans, mission statements, and job descriptions if they are available.
>
> This is an exercise you can do with colleagues in your working group in order to identify ambiguities and make sure that you are navigating from the same map. It can be particularly useful in times of transition within your organization.

Example: You are working as an advertising account executive at a *magazine publisher*. The company's mission is to publish magazines in a particular subject area. The overall objective is to provide high-quality content and make a good profit.

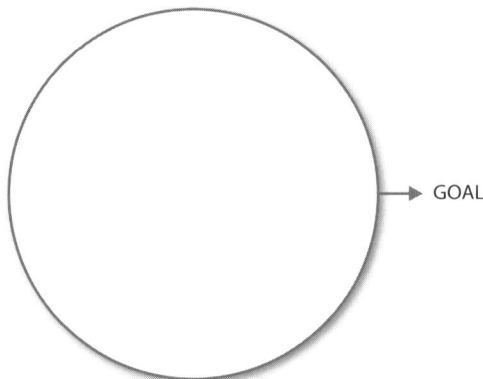

Within the publishing house, there is a *sales and marketing division* whose work helps the publisher to reach its goals by generating revenue.

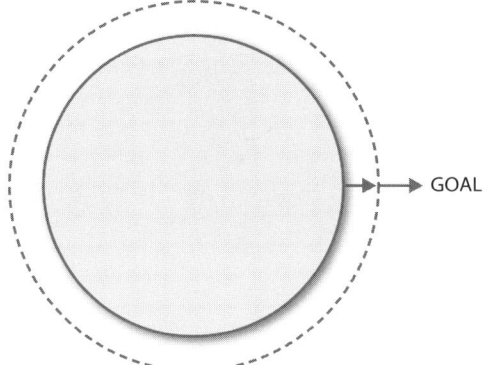

Within the sales and marketing division, there is a *sales department* responsible for all advertising sales, with a defined target for total sales.

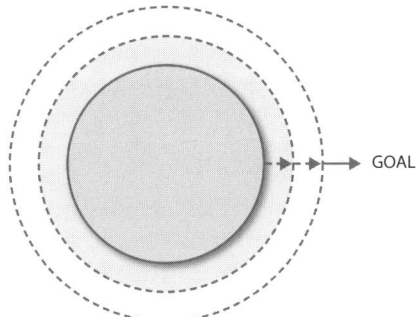

Within the sales department, there is a *team* working to sell advertising space in several magazines. The team has a collective sales target.

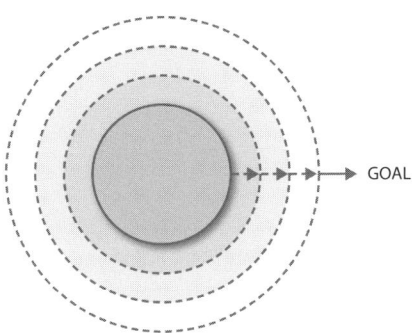

You form part of this team, and your role as *account executive* **is to contact a specified number of different companies to sell advertising space in your magazines. You have your own sales target.**

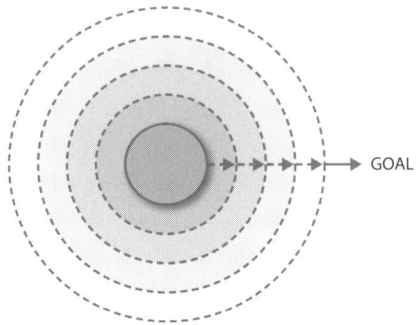

By doing this exercise, you and your colleagues create an overview of how your various organizational contexts are intended to function and connect to one another. You may also readily discover whether there is ambiguity at any level; for instance, maybe there is no defined objective for your division. Or there may be a disconnect between the levels. Do you understand how the goals of the different contexts are related to one another?

This type of analysis can help you to identify more specifically which aspects of the system's structure are already clear and usable, and which ones may require more attention and discussion.

CHAPTER 5

The importance of having a functioning filter

For our communication and other interpersonal interactions to be effective, we need to be aware of the purpose of the context we are in. Most of the time, we do have this awareness, and we are also aware that others are taking up different roles that are functional within that context. However, as we've explained, it's easy to lose this awareness at work. We often slip into behaviors and attitudes that don't belong in our professional role, and that risk eroding the necessary system boundaries. Therefore it is very useful for us to develop an internal "filter"—a permeable boundary that allows us to intellectually understand and intuitively sense which aspects of ourselves belong in our professional role and which do not. Just as a coffee filter allows water, aroma, taste, and color to pass through, while leaving out the grounds, we have the mental capacity to selectively filter out whatever is unnecessary in a particular context.

External reminders

As we step into our role at work, we are usually assisted by external markers. Every morning we drive into the same parking lot or get off at the same bus stop, and then enter a building that looks different from the house or apartment complex where we live. In some work environments, the change of context is marked by a security checkpoint. We may need to put on a name tag or identification badge. Many of us also wear different clothes at work than we do at home; when we get to our desk, we might change out of sneakers or winter boots into dress shoes. In all of these ways, our environment helps us to cross an internal, mental boundary.

Some people become very focused and collected as soon as they put on their work clothes. Others experience the same change in attitude the moment they step into their office or look at their task list for the day. Maybe just seconds before, they were daydreaming about their upcoming vacation or ruminating about a minor family problem, but those thoughts quickly fade into the background.

Distinct external environments help with role transitions

Some workplaces, including industrial sites, hospitals, and office parks, differ considerably from our environment at home. Welders, dentists, and lab technicians rarely have to think twice about the purpose of the environment they're in. Other work settings, such as counseling centers, retirement homes, or small offices, may intentionally create a home-like atmosphere to help make visitors and residents more comfortable and secure. People working in such environments, where features like comfortable armchairs and aquariums are part of a conscious strategy, may need to remind themselves of their roles more frequently. The same is true, to an even greater extent, for home health aides and personal care assistants to elderly and disabled individuals. They work in the homes of *other* people, environments that can easily evoke the attitudes, values, and behavior patterns that apply in their *own* home.

Telecommuting—a challenge

The risk of slipping out of our role as a result of the external environment is particularly clear when we work remotely. Today, more and more people are able to connect to the office and work from home, sometimes several days a week. This makes it easy to put in a load of laundry while you're on a conference call or waiting for a file to download, which may lead to a disorganized workday and divided attention. Many authors, freelancers, self-employed consultants, and others in flexible professions are aware of those risks and set strict rules for themselves concerning what they may and may not do during working hours.

Internal work

We use the term *filter* to refer collectively to all the thoughts and mental images we normally use to distinguish between different roles. The filter may operate more or less automatically, as when we change from the role of passenger on the subway to that of a consumer. Or it may operate on a more conscious level, as an internal dialogue or envisioning of our goals that helps us understand what behavior is appropriate in a given situation. The reasoning you used in the exercise in Chapter 1 (page 23) is one example of filter-based thinking.

When we're at work, a functioning filter allows our professional role to take center stage in our attention, while our other roles fade into the background. Our thoughts become focused on specific types of content, our emotions settle down to a relatively neutral state, and our behavior follows certain set patterns. Of course, there are jobs that involve improvisation, which requires you to be prepared for unexpected situations, but on the whole, most workdays are fairly predictable. It is also generally clear what is expected of us when we are on the job.

Picturing the filter

Based on the same principle as the Russian doll (as discussed in the previous chapter), the diagram on the following page provides a visual illustration of the filter and its function.

The human figure represents our overall personality (our "person"). The large circle represents our work, the context within which we exist and have our specific duties, which are represented by the smaller, halved role circle (see Chapter 2, page 30). In performing those duties, within the context of our role, we contribute to achieving the goals of the work. The arrow running from

CHAPTER 5

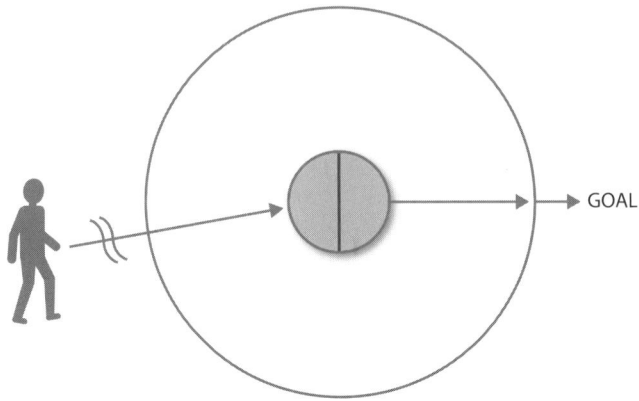

the person to the role circle illustrates that there is a connection between our personality and our professional role. Finally, between the person and the work circle is the permeable filter, the internal mechanism through which we differentiate between role and person, between the subject matter and our personal reactions.

> **EXERCISE**
>
> To increase your awareness and strengthen your filter-based thinking, try the following activity:
>
> - Copy the illustration above in a larger size, and fill in the two halves of the role circle with the elements you identified in the exercise in Chapter 2 (page 30).
>
> - Below the human figure (your "person"), make a list of your personality traits, interests, and skills. It does not need to be complete or well worded—just a number of key words that describe you as a person.
>
> - Write the headings "Let through" and "Filter out" under the filter symbol, so that you create two columns. Then look at the list you wrote down about your person, and consider which elements are useful for you in your professional capacity and

> which may need to be filtered out. You may have traits, experiences, and qualifications that fit well in certain contexts but are less useful at work, and vice versa.
> - Make a list under each heading so that you get an overall picture of what is useful and what needs to be left outside of your role.

This type of overview—a bird's eye perspective of ourselves and our function at work—is worth revisiting frequently. It's particularly useful when changes are taking place or when we switch jobs or move to a new organization. Taking a step back and looking at ourselves and our work from a distance helps us to take it less personally when things don't go the way we want them to. And if disagreements arise about the contents of our professional role, the filter model can help us assert our point of view with greater confidence and with arguments that are as objective as possible.

Requirements for a functioning filter

There are several factors that make it easier for our filter to function adequately:

- **Our personal life is reasonably crisis-free.** When there are relatively few complications in our personal lives, we function better at work. When there is nothing weighing on us, dampening our spirits, or making us oversensitive to stress and change, it's easier to separate our professional and personal roles.
- **There are clear differences between our home and work environments.** Of course, what we do at work may not necessarily be dramatically different from what we do at home, but it helps to have clear markers reminding us where we are. This is particularly important for individuals who work in a home office or work with other people in home care settings.

- **We feel like part of the group.** When there is a feeling of solidarity and mutual respect in the workplace, we are more stable emotionally and able to think more clearly and more long-term. This has a positive effect on our ability to distinguish between our role and our personal self.
- **The employer and management are clear about the purpose, mission, and goals of the work.** If we don't fully understand the larger meaning of what we're doing, it's difficult to determine which aspects of ourselves are useful and which ones we need to filter out.
- **Our direct manager is clear about roles.** Getting clear signals about what we're expected to do in our day-to-day tasks makes it easier to distinguish our person from our role. When we need to think seriously about our role, it's important to understand what we're supposed to think about; otherwise, we risk getting caught up in speculations, fears, or unrealistic ambitions.

Personal responsibility

Normally, we don't have any problem determining where our personal responsibilities lie in everyday situations. Even if we don't consciously think in terms of obligations and roles, there is no doubt about who it is that needs to sign our tax return or set our daughter straight after she decides to take up smoking. Of course, there are some dog owners who stand idly by while their unleashed pit bull terrorizes the playground, and it's not unusual to find people who keep trying to get someone else to do their job, but most of us have a built-in awareness and sense of responsibility regarding the important roles in our daily lives.

Therefore, it need not be difficult to build on the skill you already have and refine your ability to distinguish between your professional role and yourself as a person. But this doesn't just mean refraining from flooding your colleagues with detailed descriptions of your romantic life. It is to a large extent a question of working on yourself and your habitual patterns of behavior.

When you slip out of your role

The idea of working on yourself may sound vague and abstract, but it becomes clearer when we look at a concrete example: tracking your reaction pattern when you've slipped out of your role. You can increase your awareness of the circumstances in which you are easily triggered and liable to act out of impulse rather than from rational thinking.

Below are three examples in which someone has great difficulty staying in the appropriate role:

> **A manager** is participating in a meeting that is unusually slow. People are quiet and hesitant, which is out of character for this group. In an attempt to "save" the situation, the manager gives his views on the topic in an increasingly forceful voice tone, without pausing for air or leaving room for anyone else to speak. He loses himself in a long monologue, and the employees become increasingly confused. The meeting ends in a cacophony of questions about the time of the next meeting.

> **A preschool teacher** who doesn't feel comfortable being the center of attention needs to hold an informational meeting for both parents and staff. The purpose of the meeting is to introduce several new teaching strategies that he wants to start putting into practice. He is expecting a fairly sparse, intimate gathering. When he sees that the meeting is surprisingly well attended, to the point where extra chairs need to be brought in, he feels a sudden fear of failing and his heart begins to pound. He barely manages to help rearrange the room, and finds it increasingly difficult to stay focused; his mind wanders off to irrelevant thoughts about the parking ticket he received yesterday and the leaky faucet he keeps meaning to get fixed.

> **A nurses' union representative** has just had a complicated and contentious meeting with the employers' representative—a meeting that left her shaken and distraught. On her way back to the unit where her patients are waiting, she practices deep breathing while thinking to herself, "Let it go. Let it go." She envisions herself speaking calmly and thoughtfully to the worried patient in room 12, reminds herself that she is there for the good of the patients (not the other way

around), and continues to breathe deeply. By the time she reaches the unit entrance, she feels only a small remnant of agitation in the back of her mind. She is now capable of taking up her role and fulfilling the function that is expected of her in relation to the patients.

Many people recognize themselves in these examples, in one way or another. Some people can relate to the triggers, but react to them in very different ways. Instead of speaking incoherently or getting heart palpitations, they may start to feel tired, distracted, and generally out of it. Dropping out of role can mean anything from screaming rage to silent withdrawal, depending on the personal baggage we bring to the situation.

> ### EXERCISE
>
> To identify your own reaction patterns, try the following exercise (developed by Martin Ekberg, loosely based on the work of Yvonne Agazarian). Answer the following questions as honestly as you can. Take your time with each question, and take breaks between the questions so that you can concentrate and think through your answers carefully.
>
> - What are your triggers? What makes you act impulsively, without thinking? Is it a particular type of situation? Are there certain kinds of people who set you off? Or specific behaviors, like a demanding attitude, superior tone of voice, or passive silence?
> - How do you notice that you've been triggered? Do you find yourself getting distracted by certain types of thoughts? Or is there something that happens to you physically—palpitations, flushing, tremors, restlessness? Can you identify where in your body the signs are most obvious? Do you easily slip into being brusque and careless, or do you go in the opposite direction, becoming subdued, quiet, and insecure?
> - In what ways do you affect others when you're triggered? Do they become fearful, insecure, aggressive, or silent? It may be

> challenging to come up with an answer; while we can easily point out other people's shortcomings, it's often more difficult to analyze ourselves. But please try. Think about what other people have said to you and about you. Do you have teenage children? Or close friends whom you trust to tell you the truth? Ask them.
>
> - How do you handle a situation in which you've been triggered and lost your role? Do you have any constructive ways of centering yourself when you start to falter? What do you do to avoid staying stuck in an agitated or depressed frame of mind? Do you take some deep breaths, go for a walk, count to ten, or try to have an honest discussion with the person in question? Can you think of other alternatives?

This exercise can be highly beneficial when done by yourself, but may work even better in a group where the participants are open both to laughter and to serious discussion. There is a high potential for each person to recognize their own patterns in the answers that other people give. The exercise gives rise to constructive reflection, while also at times being a lot of fun as you discover how many patterns of behavior we humans tend to have in common. The ability to laugh at yourself, not taking yourself too seriously, makes the internal work of setting up a functioning filter much easier.

Interpersonal communication is so nuanced and complex that it's often best to focus first on what is simple and obvious. Identifying our more extreme patterns of reaction gives us a clear starting point for approaching those that are more subtle and elusive. It makes us more aware of the external contexts and internal reactions that can lead us to falter in our behavior and our roles. In this way, we develop an internal warning system that improves our ability to catch ourselves in time to prevent unnecessary conflict and frustration.

CHAPTER 6

What's the point of having a boss?

In every workplace, people have opinions about the manager (the "boss") and how they should behave. Often there is speculation about what this person *actually* does. Employees frequently feel that the manager spends too little time at their desk and doesn't understand what's really happening in the office. Decisions that employees feel uncomfortable or skeptical about are interpreted as showing a lack of understanding and empathy. Many employees also feel that their manager does not "see" them—a phenomenon that typically stems from unclear roles, which make it possible to expect the person in the managerial role to meet all sorts of personal needs.

There is often a lack of understanding of what a manager is and what function they perform, which easily leads to mistrust. This is true to an even greater degree for functions and roles higher up in the organization, and may result in employees closing ranks within their group or unit and perpetuating the idea that the management doesn't understand what their work involves and doesn't understand how important it is.

Leadership and the manager's role

It's important to distinguish between the manager's role and leadership. The role of manager is a position. Leadership is a relationship; it is dependent upon the acceptance and active cooperation of employees who enable a designated person to lead them.

There are managers who do not care to or are not permitted to exercise leadership—who avoid addressing contentious issues in their working groups, or whose employees don't respect their authority and don't comply with the decisions they make.

There are also leaders who don't have a formal management role. One example is a basketball coach who directs game strategy and builds skill within the team, but does not have the authority to make draft decisions or manage the team's finances. The role of team leader in an organization is also only about leadership. One person on the team is given the task of coordinating the work of the team, but is not responsible for managing the finances or the staff.

The manager's role always involves an overall responsibility for the work and its results. Even when it's an employee who makes a mistake, the manager is held ultimately responsible. A manager must focus, to varying degrees, on developing the content of the work being done, managing change, and representing the organization to the outside world. In most cases, they must also consciously exercise leadership in relation to the employees—encouraging them, supporting them, and helping them to recognize both their limitations and their potential. Leadership is about communication and the ability to facilitate learning and growth. It's one facet of the role of manager, but it's not the entire picture.

Everything that we said earlier about taking up your role also applies to the manager. If the manager does not take up their role in a functional way, this can have major consequences for the business. Among other problems, it makes it hard for the employees to take up their roles. To be functional in their role, a manager needs to follow the same principles as any employee: using those aspects of themselves that are appropriate for the context, developing a functioning filter, and distinguishing between the personal and professional areas of their lives. Where we see substantial differences between a manager and an employee is in the specific content and types of responsibilities associated with each of their roles.

The manager as boundary straddler

If you view the working group as a human system, what stands out about the manager's role is that they sit right at the edge.

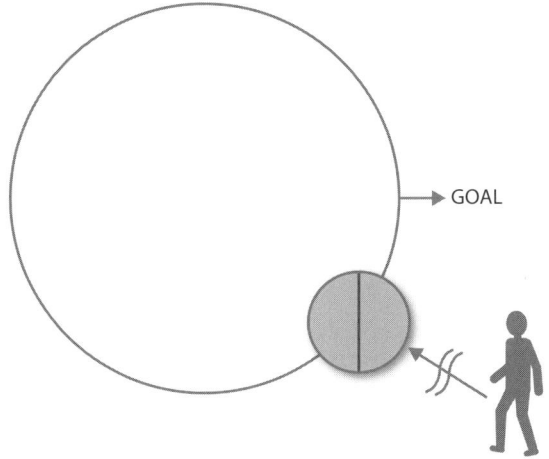

You could say that the role of managers is to straddle the boundary. Many of their responsibilities require working near the system's boundaries and managing them. Their work involves clarifying the system's mission, making sure that the right things are going on inside the system, and coordinating with other systems within the organization. In addition, managers function as channels of information from the larger organization into their working groups, and vice versa.

The precise details of this work depend in part on the working group's stage of development (see Chapter 8), but one aspect is constant: the manager has a particular focus on and responsibility for the system as a *whole*. This is necessary so that each individual employee can be in a good position to take on a functional role and be able to focus on their tasks. The manager conducts their boundary work by holding regular staff meetings and occasionally raising policy issues or doing internal monitoring, while also meeting with other managers at the same level or higher levels in the hierarchy. Another aspect of boundary work is the responsibility to stay up-to-date on the external environment by attending conferences and participating in training opportunities that are relevant to the manager's department or division.

Functional hierarchy

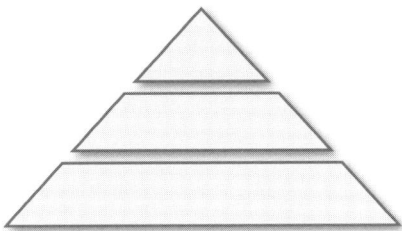

In Chapter 4, "Living Human Systems," we likened the structure of an organization to a Russian doll, or an onion. Smaller departments form part of larger divisions, which in turn are parts of even broader contexts, within a system hierarchy in which the outer circle symbolizes the outer limit of the organization. On every level, there is a manager straddling the boundary; the scope of the manager's oversight increases from level to level.

Another method of illustrating the levels of an organization is the classic pyramid model. This model has been challenged in recent years. In the 1980s and 1990s there was lots of talk of "flattening the pyramid," removing most or all middle layers of the organizational hierarchy. We wanted as short a distance as possible between manager and employee, without too many middlemen. The hard-won lesson from this experience was that while flatter organizations theoretically shorten the distance between manager and employee, giving the manager so many direct reports makes it difficult to build a meaningful relationship with all of them.

Now people are talking again about the importance of hierarchies, but this time there's an emphasis on function. The idea is that an organization should have however many levels it needs in order to operate effectively.

The pyramid metaphor illustrates the importance of having functions that have lookout points at different "heights"—both close to the ground, to catch all the details, and higher up, to gain the broader view. A functionally constructed hierarchy, with managers at strategically appropriate levels, ensures that the organization has all the important perspectives covered. In this way, a variety of different types of information become available for use within the organizational system, provided that you create useful and understandable channels of communication.

From the top, things may look completely calm, while employees at lower levels see complaints and system failures that need to be addressed. And conversely, unsuspecting "ground level" workers may be happily going about their business, making plans based on the status quo, while those higher up in the organization are aware of upcoming challenges that will have a major impact on many employees.

Thus, we can see that none of these perspectives is better or worse than any of the others. Every individual needs to take up their role, focus on the appropriate things, and share what they perceive with other levels. In addition, every level must be open to and able to manage information from the other levels. The ability to transmit and receive information in a way that minimizes misunderstandings is crucial for future success and security.

The manager's role in the hierarchy

Whenever we talk about different levels in an organization, the manager is always described as being higher up than the employees. There is good reason for this: the manager needs to have a wider perspective on the business operations, and a wider window on the outside world, than the individual employees.

Becoming a manager brings an increase in the time you're expected to devote to strategic issues, along with a decrease in the need to focus on practical day-to-day details. Your planning horizon (the length of time into the future that you are expected to plan) increases dramatically. If an employee is expected to plan weeks or months ahead, a manager at a higher level can be expected to work on visions and plans several years ahead.

One of the manager's most important tasks is communicating this wider perspective to the employees. That includes clarifying the rationales for official decisions—those that they've made by themselves, those they've made in consultation with other managers at the same level, and those that have been made higher up in the hierarchy. This work takes place in parallel with the manager's ongoing practical leadership responsibilities.

Considerations for the employee

As an employee, you have a responsibility to understand and keep in mind that your manager has a role to play in working toward the goals of your organization. When you realize this, it becomes easier to make reasonable and relevant requests of them.

> **Two coworkers** have had difficulty getting along for quite some time. The conflict stems partly from different opinions about how the work should be done, but is partly personal as well. They both disapprove of each other's personal life choices, and both are very hot-tempered. The result is that coffee breaks often degenerate into petty arguments between these two people, while their other coworkers look on uncomfortably.
>
> Neither of the opposing parties has any interest in what the manager thinks about their situation. They are so caught up in the conflict that they don't realize it's affecting other people and having a detrimental effect on their work.
>
> The others do not speak up; they just hope the manager will discover the problem and make everything all right. Some of them imagine that if only the manager found out, the troublemakers would get the reprimand they deserve. Others see the manager as a weakling who lacks the courage to confront the issue.
>
> Nobody wants to be the one to tell the manager. No one wants to be a tattletale. Some people feel that the manager ought to see what's happening anyway—he should be able to, for all the money he makes.

This example illustrates a common situation: the employees aren't clear on the manager's function and don't give him an opportunity to exercise leadership; they don't give him the information he'd need to address the conflict in the context of the group's goals. Instead, the conflict continues against a background of vague, unspoken expectations of what the manager should be doing. Of course, it's also possible that the manager has contributed to the problem by being unclear and passive in his leadership.

As a member of a team or working group, you need to be aware of the special function and role of the manager. You also need to be aware of your more irrational expectations, particularly in times of change, and to nurture a task-oriented relationship with the leader. Staying focused on the task does not mean appeasing the leader or staying silent about problems you experience at work. On the contrary, a task orientation makes it possible to bring up difficult topics with your manager in a constructive way.

The employee/manager relationship

It's common knowledge that relationships with people in positions of leadership or authority can be very complicated. Our experiences of leaders are shaped by our parents, teachers, sports coaches, and other adults we encounter while growing up—and those experiences are not always positive. We often interpret a manager's behavior and decisions through the lens of what has happened to us in the past, particularly during periods of stressful change.

You can help to create a functional relationship with your manager by basing your feedback and requests on facts, rather than speculation. It's also important to avoid seeing decisions that you're unhappy or uncomfortable with as personal insults, and to realize that the manager needs to spend a lot of time on long-term strategic planning and analysis of the external environment.

EXERCISE

Try the following thought experiment as an exercise in differentiating between your personal expectations of your manager and the more objective requirements determined by your function at work and the context you're in. (If you're a manager, think about your immediate superior.)

1. Thinking only about yourself and your own personal needs, what type of manager/leader would you like? Write down the characteristics, behaviors, and attitudes that appeal to you, without regard to your specific line of work or professional role.

2. Now, take your personal preferences out of the equation and focus only on your professional role, the context you work in, and the goals of your organization. What type of manager/leader is required? Try to take an outside perspective, as if you were thinking about somebody else's workplace. Write down the characteristics, behaviors, and attitudes that would be functional in the role of manager.

3. Compare your two different responses, and reflect upon the similarities and differences. Is there a big difference between the manager you would love to have and the leadership that is actually necessary at your workplace? Is your communication with your manager colored by your own personal needs, leading you to relate to them in a way that isn't functional within your work context? Does your more objective description of the type of leadership needed at your workplace correspond with how things actually function right now?

CHAPTER 7

Meetings, meetings, and more meetings

Most people enjoy socializing with other people, interacting with family, friends, and work colleagues. Without this need to be a part of a group and a broader context, humans would not have developed into the beings that we are today. It's through our shared communication and experiences that ideas are born. Our time together provides an opportunity to build off each other's points of view, grow as individuals, and develop as groups.

Unfortunately, these interactions are not always as functional or constructive as they could be. Over the course of our lives, we all develop characteristic patterns of interacting and communicating with others. You can think of these as habitual roles (see Chapter 1). When we communicate in a spontaneous and unreflective manner, it's those habitual patterns that drive our behavior. We provide information if and when we feel like it, and we often fail to consider how the people around us might be affected or whether the information is going where it really needs to go.

Without well-thought-out, goal-directed communication, there's a risk that our energy, ideas, and attention will drift around without direction or focus. Therefore, all workplaces need forums that facilitate a more conscious, structured exchange of information and help us direct our messages in a purposeful way.

Why we need meetings

The most compelling reason for having meetings at work is the need to share information. Meetings are a place where people's facts, experiences, proposals, perspectives, and opinions get expressed and responded to. This shared knowledge forms a good foundation for decision making and contributes to reaching the group's goals.

As we discussed in Chapter 4 ("Living Human Systems"), the process of taking in new information and integrating it with what we already know is of fundamental importance for development. Within an organization, this means that discussions about differences and opposing opinions are essential for us to move forward in our work. But without a firm meeting structure, we often can't take advantage of differences. Feelings, reactions, and ideas get thrown out in such a disorganized way that we never get anywhere.

Anyone who's tried to build a wildflower garden can see the parallels. If you allow all the plants to grow freely, you'll never achieve the result you want. After a while, the area will become a tangled mess, taken over by a few plants that grow at the expense of all the others. It will be impossible to get a coherent sense of the garden as a whole, and you'll need a machete to get through.

A wildflower garden requires more work and structure than you might think. Some plants need to be cut back and others helped to grow so that together, they provide a harmonious overall impression, while at the same time individual plants are allowed to express their unique characteristics.

In the same way, it takes thought and effort to create functional meetings in which it feels natural to put forward your opinions, listen to other people, and have open discussions.

Saying the right thing in the wrong context

In all too many workplaces, there is a jumble of sensible meetings, inexplicable meetings, and informal meetings where decisions are made despite the fact that not everyone who ought to be present is there.

When important discussions and exchanges of information are not regulated in a purposeful way, the door is open for all sorts of communication channels (and communication blockages) to form throughout the organization. Our tendency to relate to each other based on personal preferences and habitual ways of communicating takes over, and this leads to a lot of wasted energy.

It's common for people to have important information, ideas, and opinions that are highly relevant to their work, but express them to the wrong person, at the wrong time, or in the wrong place. *The wrong person* may be somebody who understands the concern but doesn't have any power to act in the matter. *The wrong time* may mean bringing up an important issue at 4:20 p.m. on a Friday afternoon. *The wrong place* may mean discussing an issue at the coffee machine, in the hallway, or on the elevator, and staying silent when that issue comes up in a meeting. The result may be a feeling of not being heard, or not having one's opinions taken seriously, when in fact the problem is that the information was introduced in an inappropriate context.

Frequently, precious meeting time is consumed by issues that are not a priority in the agenda, or even on the agenda at all.

> **An executive team meeting** with the goal of reaching consensus on a joint decision degenerates into a dispute about the company's mission and vision.

> **An information session** about ongoing construction work turns into a debate about the rationale behind the renovations.

> **A working group** holds a meeting to compose a letter to their supervisor requesting more information about the details of a new position that's being created, but spends the whole time angrily speculating about the motives behind some recent incomprehensible decisions made by the management.

Those types of unstructured, unreflective approaches also open the way for communication to be influenced by a wide variety of personal idiosyncrasies. These may include a fear of conflict or a tendency to bury one's head in the sand; a person who is uncomfortable with conflict might call in sick to avoid a meeting where there is a high risk of unpleasantness due to the lack of clear direction or control. Others may respond by telling lots of jokes, making one sarcastic comment after another, or getting caught up in pessimistic worries about the future. All of these make it impossible to have a productive discussion.

In such cases, the leader has a responsibility to establish the norms for communicating important information.

> **A CEO leading a large organization** was proud of how his decision-making process was working. He avoided lengthy back-and-forth discussions in meetings, and instead dealt with issues spontaneously, as they arose. He described himself as being unusually efficient and effective, pointing out how he solved problems in one-on-one conversations or initiated important new projects during a coffee break or in casual chats in the hallway.
>
> At the same time, the experience of the employees in the organization was one of great uncertainty and stress. Rumors spread about hidden agendas. Many people were on constant alert for potential conflict and ambushes, while others worried about being left behind without really understanding why.

When the lines of communication are unclear, or are implied rather than explicitly stated, this may lead to a situation in which

- employees are unclear about the purpose and goals of the organization, resulting in a poor working climate
- employees are unsure of their roles and wonder whether what they're doing is right, or if there are other things they're supposed to be doing
- important information fails to reach everyone who's affected by it
- many decisions make no sense to the employees
- the decision-making process becomes a mystery
- frequent misunderstandings and errors occur (think of what happens in the children's game of Telephone)
- unnecessary conflicts grow, while necessary conflicts stay hidden

- employees form inaccurate impressions of what the managers and top executives really do
- people at the management level are ill-informed about the day-to-day reality of the employees

So how can we structure our interactions so that information gets across accurately and effectively, in a way that's functional for the organization?

Communication and plumbing

To have a functional exchange of information in the workplace, we need a clear and usable structure indicating when, where, and how different issues get discussed. We can understand how this structure works with the help of a simple analogy.

The information channels of an organization can be likened to a plumbing system. Developing functional lines of communication is like doing a plumbing installation.

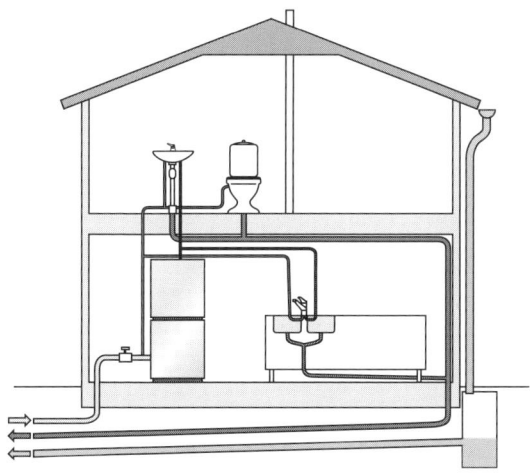

In a house, we have different pipes for water and sewage. The pipes need to be connected in such a way that the right contents get to the right pipe, and they need to be appropriately sized based on the amount of fluid each pipe needs to transport. When there is a blockage in a pipe, it needs to get cleaned out to avoid unpleasant consequences.

Similarly, in a workplace, we need different forums to handle the exchange of various types of information. These forums need to be clearly defined and understood by everyone involved. They also need to be appropriately sized—having the right frequency and duration to make them useful. It makes no sense to hold a 15-minute meeting to discuss a complex strategic issue (the pipe is far too narrow), but 15 minutes may be sufficient for a morning check-in to review upcoming tasks for the day (the pipe diameter is correct).

It's also important for everyone to know how the pipe continues. What happens next with the information that is being discussed? Is it clear *whether* and *how* any next steps will be taken? Is it clear how any feedback is supposed to be given?

There may be blockages in the pipe that cause the information to stop at one level. People may not know where to direct the information, or they may forget that what is obvious to them may not be so obvious to others. They may also be uncomfortable passing on information that is not to their advantage. A team leader may be reluctant to inform their manager about problems within their team for fear that it will have a negative impact on their position or career.

When formal forums do not work properly, information finds its own way around an organization. It leaks out of the system, making it much more arbitrary what information comes forward, and whom it reaches. The information flow will be governed by informal forces: who listens to whom, who is the most dominant, and who has the most highly placed personal contacts.

Meetings: function-structure-person

It's quite common for employees and managers to sit through meetings that have no clear agenda and no longer fulfill a function. Sometimes there is a stated goal for a meeting, but it has little or no relationship to what actually gets discussed. Other meetings are mainly a forum for personal chitchat and gossip about the job. All of this wastes energy and easily leads to frustration and a general mistrust of meetings.

To enable all of our meetings to become the forums of information exchange and development that they're intended to be, we need to set clear guidelines for each one. One way of creating such guidelines is to look at the *function* of the meeting: What is the purpose of the meeting? What is it intended to achieve? What need is the meeting supposed to fulfill?

> **A team of salespeople** who mainly work on their own, independently from one another, meet up periodically to provide each other with peer support and discuss issues that call for a unified approach.

> **Staff members at a nursing home,** who work different shifts, meet regularly as a group to exchange information on the residents and prevent any misunderstandings about the individuals' needs, health status, and plans of care.

> **A symphony orchestra** meets with its artistic director to obtain information about the program for the following season.

Once the function of a meeting is clear, the next step is establishing an appropriate *structure* to support that function, which will make it easier to achieve whatever you're trying to achieve. Meeting structure includes factors such as

- Duration: How long should the meeting be?
- Frequency: How often should the meeting be held?
- Agenda: What issues should be discussed?
- Management: What type of leadership does the meeting require?
- Participation: In what ways are the participants expected to contribute?

In addition, there are practical considerations that need to be sorted out, such as finding a good time and location for the meeting.

There is no magic prescription for a good meeting structure other than it must support the function of the meeting. All too often, this is not the case; structures get created based on personal wishes or old habits and traditions, and we forget to clarify what the goal is.

Finally, it's important to determine which *people* are going to participate. This too should be based on the function of the meeting, rather than on established traditions or a general desire to be polite or inclusive. In workplaces where personal agendas have a powerful influence, it's common for individuals to get upset if they're not included in certain meetings, sometimes interpreting this as a sign that they're not well liked. But the rationale for meeting participation is not personal; it's based on whether or not you have something crucial to contribute, given your role.

By sorting out issues of function, structure, and person, you create the basic conditions for a useful exchange of information. If you continue to monitor these factors on a regular basis—checking to see whether the meeting is still functional, the structure still works, and the right people are still in the right places—there's a good chance that the group's energy and resources will stay focused in a constructive way.

Small action—great effect

A good rule of thumb is that the leader of a meeting *always* introduces *every* meeting by reminding the participants of the reason why they're meeting, what the time frame is, what's on the agenda, and what the intended outcome is (e.g., a specific plan, decision, or action). While this may seem like stating the obvious, it goes a long way toward helping each participant to focus their attention and adopt a functional attitude toward the task at hand.

Another important consideration is making sure that the room layout and seating arrangement are appropriate for the purpose of the meeting. In a group discussion, all participants must be able to see each other. An arrangement that allows everyone to maintain eye contact without straining their neck facilitates open communication and an easy, fluid exchange of ideas. If the meeting is an information session in which everyone's attention is directed toward the front of the room, theater-style seating is often preferable. If the agenda includes a mix of these two formats, you can start with the information session and then take a five-minute break, let people stretch their legs, and move the furniture around so that all participants can talk to each other easily.

There are many good reasons to take a close look at the structure of our meetings and strive to make them as effective as possible. One motivating factor is the psychological effect on employees: the ambiguity of having unstructured meetings without a clear goal tends to contribute to fatigue and apathy at work. Better meetings also improve the overall working climate and allow lunches and coffee breaks to serve the function they're intended to serve—providing a time for relaxation, laughter, and socialization. Of course, we still might occasionally have an urgent issue come up and intrude into our leisure time, and that's perfectly fine, so long as the exception never becomes the rule.

CHAPTER 8
Looking through the lens of group development

As we attempt to take up our professional roles in a functional way, it is extremely helpful to understand the basic processes of group dynamics. Whether we're working as a member of a team or as its leader, we sometimes need to change our approach so that it's in keeping with the developmental stage the group is in.

We generally don't think much about it, but all of us have a long personal history with group dynamics. Throughout our lives, each of us participates in many different types of groups: our family, classes at school, circles of friends, sports teams, clubs, and so on. So when we begin thinking about the development of teams or organizations, we have more relevant experience to draw upon than we might imagine.

An integrated model of group development

Recent research in group psychology has clearly shown that different types of groups, including work teams, progress through a number of developmental phases—*from* an initial phase characterized by insecurity and a focus on getting to know each other, *through* a period of exchanging and clashing over differing opinions, *up until* a stage where the members clearly understand their roles and functions and can work in an organized, structured way to reach their goals.

Another way of understanding that process is from the point of view of the group members. When we join together to form a new group, we start out from a self-focused perspective in which emotions and relationships take center stage. Eventually, this focus on the self starts to give way to a broader awareness of the purpose and goals of our work. Finally, we reach a point where our interactions are predominantly task-oriented and we take up our roles with the attitudes and competencies that are useful in the context we're in.

Psychologist and researcher Susan Wheelan has developed an integrated model of group development that clarifies this progression in a very useful way. She divides a group's life into four stages; these stages follow one another in sequence, but a group can also move backward in its development, as a result of external influences or other factors. At each stage, the group must accomplish specific tasks before it can continue to develop.

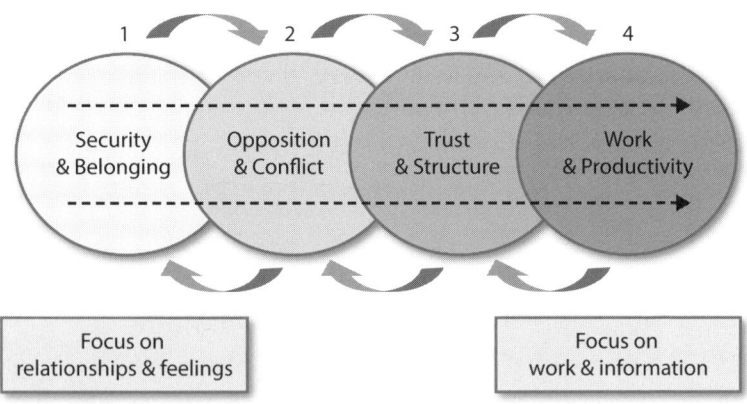

Note: Susan Wheelan refers to Stage 1 as Dependency & Inclusion and Stage 2 as Counterdependency & Fight, but when her book *Creating Effective Teams* was translated into Swedish, these terms were changed to the Swedish equivalents of Security & Belonging and Opposition & Conflict. We like this simpler, more accessible terminology, and chose to preserve it—with her permission—for this English translation.

Stage 1: Security and belonging

In newly formed groups where the members don't know each other very well, communication is usually tentative, polite, and cautious. It's likely that some people will feel a little insecure and suspicious of others in the group. Of course, there may be one or two individuals who just charge ahead with no regard to the delicacy of the situation, and as a result are perceived as forward or insensitive. Most of us, however, tend to occupy ourselves with trying to figure out what the other group members are like. Discreetly, we attempt to gauge whether we will feel comfortable in the group, and whether the group can give us a feeling of security and belonging.

At this stage, the group focuses on visible similarities. Parents of young children, fans of the same sports teams, and individuals with the same educational background smile appreciatively at each other, without knowing whether they'll actually be able to work together well. People breathe a sigh of relief when others in the group laugh at the same jokes or express similar interests or points of view.

Obviously Stage 1 groups get some work done as well, but the communication and tasks take place against the background of a desire for security and belonging. In order to feel comfortable working together, we need to find common ground. This first stage of development lays the foundation for the security and solidarity that the group will need when working conditions change or when conflicts arise.

Stage 1 groups require a stable, reliable leader who can clearly answer the members' questions and who doesn't expect any more independent behavior from them than is possible during this initial phase. Leaders at this stage must recognize that the group members are dependent on them and may idealize them from time to time. They must also respect the cautiousness of the group's communication, and not expect everyone to be open and direct from day one.

Once the needs for security and belonging have been sufficiently satisfied, it becomes easier for everyone to directly state what they're thinking. This is an important step forward; in order for the group to take advantage of all of its available energy and resources, people's opinions and values must be openly expressed. As this starts to happen, the differences between the members of the group become more evident, which allows the group to move on to the next developmental stage.

Stage 2: Opposition and conflict

Most people feel uncomfortable dealing with conflict. However, the only way a group can develop and move out of Stage 1 is by going through a period in which opinions clash and the roles of both the members and the leader get hashed out through honest, goal-oriented discussions. The group needs to define itself, and this will inevitably lead to a certain amount of friction.

In Stage 2, questions about meeting structures, areas of responsibility, and the role of the leader get discussed and debated. Individual members put forward their own ideas and visions of how they want to work, what they think the manager ought to do, or what the focus of certain meetings should be. This injects a burst of energy into the group. At the same time, the tension created by the clash of differing opinions makes it easy to lose a sense of objectivity and instead get drawn into personal conflicts, which can become quite heated.

When a group does a poor job of managing Stage 2 dynamics, this leads to rumors, exaggerations, and a lack of nuanced understanding. Reality gets divided into very simple categories: right vs. wrong, good vs. bad, us vs. them. We find ourselves constantly at the ready to defend ourselves or launch an attack. Often our communication becomes sharp and antagonistic, and we misinterpret what others are trying to communicate to us. Our frustrations get directed toward one or more scapegoats, either within or outside the group. (The leader of the group is the most common target.) If we fail to understand that there are other, more constructive ways of handling conflicts, we risk slipping into a state of pessimism and hopelessness.

During this stage, we need to remember that the push and pull of conflicting opinions is not negative; on the contrary, this is precisely what needs to happen to clarify the structures and procedures that will guide our work together as a group. The leader, for their part, needs to communicate calmly and clearly, with their feet firmly planted on the ground, throughout any friction and turbulence that arises. If attacks are directed at them, they must be able to respond constructively and avoid taking offense or retaliating. They need to allow and encourage open discussion and debate, while also reminding the group of its mission, its goals, and the larger context surrounding its work.

Stage 3: Trust and structure

Once a group has created clear structures and procedures, together with a functional system of roles and responsibilities, it enters Stage 3. The general sense of safety that was created in Stage 1 has developed into mutual trust that is grounded in specific experiences with each person, in the context of their professional role. At this stage, disagreements and friction are handled primarily on the basis of people's roles, rather than their personalities or personal preferences. Differences are viewed as assets rather than annoyances, individuals' unique competencies are seen resources for the group, and meetings are generally well structured and organized. If the group had a tough time in Stage 2, there's a particular appreciation for work-related jokes that have no hostile overtones.

As a group gains a solid foundation of trust and structure, the members become more self-sufficient and capable of handling a great deal of work on their own. The leader is better able to assign tasks and delegate decision-making authority, and can play more of a supportive (rather than directive) role.

Stage 4: Work and productivity

The final, mature stage of development is focused on refining or fine-tuning the working climate and structures that were established in Stage 3. Individual initiatives and independent work are well coordinated with the activities of the group as a whole. People make a conscious effort to give each other constructive feedback, and have found ways of communicating and sharing information that minimize the risk of misunderstanding. The group has become a high-performing team, in every respect. Team members genuinely look forward to being at work, and their meetings and conversations fill the team with constructive energy.

Now, when mistakes happen or things don't go as well as expected, people don't take it personally or look for scapegoats. Instead, they examine the entire system, with an understanding that the problem is of common concern to all of them.

Meanwhile, the leader is able to devote a large proportion of their working hours to analyzing the external environment and engaging in long-term planning. In a sense, they have become less separate from the rest of the group; they function as an expert member who specializes in strategic decision making in relation to an ever-changing environment. At the same time, the leader can also motivate and encourage the other members, based on their overall understanding of the character and resources of the group.

Few working groups ever reach this stage of development, and it can be difficult to remain here. There is a great risk of becoming complacent and ignoring factors that might disturb what's become a comfortable way of doing things. Thus, even in a high-performing team, it's necessary to have ongoing discussions about everyone's roles and responsibilities. The challenge is to keep this dialogue alive.

Not always a linear progression

Many working groups have been in existence for a long time. Employees come and go due to retirement, maternity leave, new hires, and changes in the organization. This means that development is not always linear. The group may temporarily fall back into an earlier stage, or subgroups within the larger group may at times function at higher or lower levels. It is important for leaders to be aware of this and be able to adapt their leadership style accordingly.

The employee's role as a group member

A basic understanding of how groups function and develop, combined with knowing which stage one's own group is in, can help the members to behave more effectively. Just as the leader needs to behave differently depending on the stage of the group, the members too have a responsibility to contribute to the group's continued development. There are several different ways to do this.

One important ground rule is to let go of the focus on yourself and *identify as a member of the team*. You can't be a functional part of a work group and at the same time buy into the illusion that you are completely self-sustaining, with no need for other people.

In addition, it's essential to avoid placing blame solely on individuals, and instead *interpret problems as group problems*. Issues such as disorganized meetings, unclear decision-making procedures, or a negative atmosphere are shared concerns, and working toward their solution is everyone's responsibility.

Group members can also facilitate the work by *initiating discussions about the distribution of roles and responsibilities within the group*. Simply getting a discussion going about issues of collaboration and communication can provide a sense of control and context. By working as a group to stay conscious of these concerns and correct mistakes and misunderstandings early, before they escalate, you can prevent the need for intervention by managers or consultants.

A fly on the wall

The best way to assess a group's developmental stage, based on the model described in this chapter, is to use a scientifically validated test called the GDQ (Group Development Questionnaire) that was specifically designed for this purpose. But it's also possible to make many relevant observations on your own and come up with a reasonable guess about what stage of development your group is currently in.

> **EXERCISE**
>
> *Please read through the chapter several times before doing this exercise.*
>
> Observe your own working group. Imagine that you're a fly on the wall—you hear everything and see everything, but nobody can see you. Experiment with this in several different ways:
>
> - Choose a day when you can distance yourself somewhat from the conversations and meetings that you normally participate in. Pay close attention to people's voice tones, the contents of the communication, and how you conduct your meetings. Does it seem obvious to you what stage of development your group is in, or is it more subtle and elusive?
> - When significant shifts occur within a group, it's common for concerns related to security and belonging to re-emerge, even if the group has been in existence for a long time. If you've recently gone through a major organizational change, or if there are new people in the group, see whether you can detect signs of such concerns from one or more members.
> - Are you lucky enough to have recently joined a newly formed project team in which you and the other members already know each other, but have never worked together so closely? This gives you a fantastic opportunity to follow the stages of group development from beginning to end, provided you don't get stuck in the opposition and conflict stage.
> - Notice whether there are certain activities or periods of time during which the group seems to be operating in Stage 3 or 4, while in other contexts and situations, performance declines and you get stuck in a mixture of Stages 1 and 2.

Using Wheelan's model to study the communication patterns of a group gives us much to discover and reflect upon—including how individuals adopt different, more or less functional roles; the problems that can arise when roles need to change or evolve; and how important it is to look at ourselves as a group, not just as individual people.

CHAPTER 9
Thought as a tool

While it's possible to think about our professional role in a fairly neutral way, sometimes we've invested so much of ourselves in that role that it's difficult to shift our thoughts and attitudes in the way that's expected of us. Often, it's our habitual patterns of thinking that create obstacles and inner resistance when something needs to change at work. As we described in Chapter 2, staying in our role requires adaptability, and this applies as much to our thinking as to our behavior. When the external environment changes, a behavior that once was useful may become ineffective. In the same way, a pattern of thought that worked for us in the past can become a liability if we stubbornly cling to it when the context requires a new way of thinking. There are also some very common ways of thinking that tend to be unproductive in any context, such as rehashing blameful stories about the past or catastrophizing about the future.

Therefore, if we want to move away from self-focused behavior and act more in harmony with our role at work, we need to tighten up our thinking and align it with the tasks at hand. This means critically examining how we interpret certain situations—how we draw conclusions and make decisions about what we observe and experience. The exercise at the end of Chapter 5 serves as a basic foundation for that type of analysis. In the sections that follow, we'll delve deeper into this issue.

Past, present, and future

As human beings we have an incredible ability to control our thinking. First and foremost, we can think in three different time

CHAPTER 9

frames: we can remember things that happened in the past, we can perceive things that are happening right now, and we can imagine things that may or may not happen in the future. This is primarily a good thing; it helps us to move forward, especially in the workplace. If we lacked the ability to look backward and evaluate past efforts, or to plan future projects, we'd have a hard time getting anything accomplished.

But the flexibility of our thinking also has a flip side. Sometimes, we feel and act as though something is happening *right now*, when in reality it either happened in the past or hasn't happened yet. We get fixated on an unsuccessful organizational change that happened a long time ago, or we work ourselves up into a frenzy about negotiations that are still weeks away.

Wherever we find ourselves—at our desk, in a meeting, or at home in front of the television—we often run into trouble when we dwell on what happened in the past or might happen in the future, instead of noticing and relating to what we can experience in the present.

> **A single mother** has finally sat down in front of the television with her two children on a Friday night to watch a Disney movie. The dishwasher rumbles in the background, there's a glass of red wine on the coffee table, and the kids are lounging on the couch in their pajamas. The only thing left to do is brush their teeth later—or maybe they can just fall asleep where they are, while she watches the romantic comedy she's been wanting to see. Everything is quiet and peaceful.
>
> Then suddenly she realizes that she still hasn't arranged childcare for the following Saturday, when she's been invited out to dinner with friends. It doesn't take long for her thoughts to get taken over by memories of past difficulties she's had in finding a babysitter, which starts to seem like an insurmountable task.
>
> She loses touch with the relaxed atmosphere of the present moment and is unable to experience how good things are right now.

> **An employee** is on his way to the first staff meeting with his department's new manager. He knows very little about this person but thinks back to his previous manager, whom he didn't get along with. The closer he gets to the meeting room, the more absorbed he becomes in memories of various confrontations he had with his old boss.

> By the time he steps into the room and greets the new manager, he's in a rather gloomy, suspicious frame of mind, which in turn leads the manager to feel a bit uneasy around him.

Facts and interpretations

In addition to thinking in different time frames, in any given context we can also switch between paying attention to hard facts and adding on our own interpretations.

Our interpretive frames act as colored glasses through which we view the events occurring around us and within ourselves. The coloring of the glasses is created by the conclusions and generalizations we've taken away from our past experiences. To some extent, this perspective is necessary. Generalizations from the past enable us to make quick, overall judgments of different situations, which helps us understand what's happening and act in a sensible way. But we also need to remember that those are just our interpretations, not absolute facts. Sometimes our interpretations are wrong; our conclusions from the past were incorrect, or they don't apply to the situation we're in now, and we need to adjust our behavior accordingly. Failing to recognize this possibility, and instead perceiving our incorrect interpretations as facts, can cause great difficulties for us.

> **Karen is so quiet in this meeting. She's usually so chatty.**
>
> *Interpretation:* I wonder if she doesn't like what I said about the new business plan. It's so irritating when people can't just be straightforward and honest. Of course she'll probably bitch about it to Kevin later.
>
> *Fact:* Karen is dealing with a serious personal problem that she hasn't had a chance to mention to any of her colleagues. She knows that her silence will probably lead to speculation, but she can't decide whether it's appropriate to raise the issue in this meeting; there's been so much talk lately about how important it is to separate personal and professional roles.

CHAPTER 9

Here and now

In order to be able to solve problems and make good decisions, we need to be present in the moment and base our reasoning primarily on facts, rather than interpretations. The more complex or turbulent a situation is—for instance, when our organization is undergoing a major change—the more important it is to focus on the here and now and collect the facts we need to make realistic plans for the future. But often, paradoxically, we do just the opposite, losing ourselves in self-focused interpretations and oversimplifications about what's happened or what lies ahead.

A model for understanding our thought patterns

The following model illustrates the different types of thinking generated by the time frame and type of information we focus on.

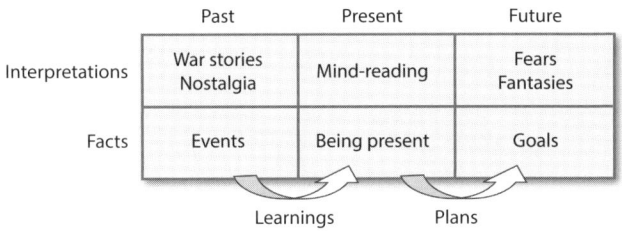

Loosely based on the work of Kurt Lewin and Yvonne Agazarian

The columns represent the dimension of time, capturing the difference between looking backward, looking forward, and focusing on the here and now. On the top row are our subjective, often one-sided and generalizing interpretations of reality. On the bottom row are more reality-based patterns of thinking, which are capable of accommodating the paradoxes and unpredictability of our existence. In the remainder of this chapter, we'll describe each of these thought patterns in greater detail.

Interpretations of the past: War stories and nostalgia

When we travel back in time through our interpretations of the past, we often do so with negative overtones in the form of *war stories*. These are emotional stories about what has failed to work, whose fault it is, and how either our working group or we as an individual have suffered as a result.

- It's always been like this. Dysfunction is woven into the very fabric of this organization.
- We learned to stop bringing up issues. Nobody ever listens to this department.
- The last reorganization ruined everything!

These characterizations frequently contain a grain of truth, but the generalizing interpretation and emotional charge turn them into war stories. War stories cast a dark shadow over the present and can generate a feeling of hopelessness that keeps discussions mired in pessimism. It may feel as though we're processing an issue, but actually we're stuck in quicksand; the more we talk, the deeper we sink into a negative, fatalistic point of view.

Interpretations of the past that have a more positive spin can be categorized as *nostalgia*.

- Things were so much better in the old days!
- Remember the manager we used to have? He knew how to get things done.
- In the past, employees used to have respect for their superiors. They weren't so arrogant and impertinent.

Idealizing the past is often used as a way of criticizing the current situation. We emphasize how bad it is right now by exaggerating how good things used to be. Just like war stories, nostalgia can prevent constructive efforts to solve problems and make decisions.

CHAPTER 9

Interpretations of the future: Fears and fantasies

Another type of thinking that can get us into trouble is worrying about things that have not yet happened, and may never happen. There's a famous quotation on this topic (frequently, though erroneously, attributed to Mark Twain):

> "I am an old man and have known a great many troubles, but most of them never happened."

This witty remark captures a deep psychological truth. A great deal of human suffering results not from actual events in the world, but from our own thinking—and particularly from our thoughts about the future. We feel anxiety, uneasiness, or fear as a consequence of thoughts such as:

- It will never work!
- I know I'll make a fool of myself.
- The new management will ruin everything!

Fantasies and positive speculations are the flip side of fears. They may not be as paralyzing as constant worrying, but they can still prevent us from getting a realistic perspective on the future. Some fantasies tend to turn us into passive spectators, discouraging us from being as active and involved as we could be:

- As soon as the new management team is in place, everything will be fine.
- Once we move to the beautiful new office space, everyone will be so much happier, and they'll forget about all these petty conflicts.
- Just give it another month or two. This problem will take care of itself.

Both fantasies and fears can lead us to place responsibility for future events outside of ourselves. We end up sitting in passive anticipation of the terrible thing that's going to happen or the perfect solution that's going to magically appear.

Interpretations of the present: Mind-reading

Even when we focus on what is happening right now, we still run the risk of misinterpretations and erroneous judgments. Mind-reading is thinking that we can know what someone else thinks, feels, or wants, even though they haven't told us—as though those things are hidden behind what the person actually says or does, and we can "read between the lines." Far too often, we act as though our mind-reads are true. In reality, sometimes they're accurate, and sometimes they're not. Therefore it's important to test our mind-reads frequently, checking to see whether our ideas about the other person are right or wrong. Otherwise, we can easily jump to conclusions based on incomplete information, leading to misunderstandings and the spread of rumors.

A manager needs to explain something to her team. She stands up, walks to the whiteboard, and begins drawing diagrams and giving explanations. The employees remain seated.

These are observable facts that everyone can see and agree on. However, those facts can be interpreted in completely different ways:

1) The manager must be drawing those diagrams for instructional purposes, trying to make some complex ideas easier to understand.

2) Typical! The manager takes every opportunity to look down on the employees. Now she's showing her power and disrespect by making them all sit passively while she lectures to them.

3) Poor woman! The manager's back pain must be acting up again, so she's taking the first opportunity to stand and give her back a rest.

These different interpretations will lead to very different feelings and behaviors. Each interpretation is entirely possible, but we can't know which one is true (if any) until we compare our mind-read with reality.

CHAPTER 9

Learning from the past

As we think back to events from the past, and particularly to past mistakes and failures, it can be challenging to make use of them in a constructive way. We need to look beyond our war stories and other oversimplifications to get a clearer understanding of what's actually happened.

Reality is complex and multifaceted. When we get some distance and look at our previous work experience from a more objective perspective, we can start to perceive the subtleties and gray areas; instead of a single, fixed narrative, we can see multiple explanations for why things turned out the way they did. To gain this perspective, we need to take a broader view of the world, including an understanding of how the situation and surrounding context appeared at that time—not just in 20/20 hindsight. No good can come from thinking of ourselves as victims of circumstance or ruminating about others who we believe have wronged us. We learn the most from our own misinterpretations and questionable decisions, not from those of others. When we think through our experiences in a systematic way, instead of accumulating a random collection of war stories and fantasies, it gets easier to learn from the past and make smart decisions in the present.

Planning for the future

In addition to learning from the past, we also need to be able to plan for the future. We need to have things to look forward to and goals to strive toward. Our need to experience our existence as reasonably predictable must be satisfied. At the same time, it's impossible to truly know anything about the future. What will happen a decade, a year, or even a minute from now is unknowable; beyond the fact that sooner or later, our life on earth will end, there's nothing else we can know for certain. This is a challenge that we have to come to terms with, in all areas of our lives—including our work.

This may be easier said than done. In times of change, it's not unusual to hear demands for *guarantees* that the change will go as planned and achieve the expected results. Nobody can promise that. But we can make careful assessments of the current situation to increase the chances that the change will be successful, and then be sure to evaluate the results we actually get.

In reality, we always live on the threshold of the unknown, even in the most familiar, everyday contexts. If we can remind ourselves of this in our professional role and base our actions on the facts that exist in the present, we can set goals and plan for the future in a way that is as realistic as possible.

Being present

We view the present through the lens of our own biases and assumptions, but with the help of a nuanced view of the past and the future, the lens becomes less distorted, and this helps give us a better view.

> **A management team** has for years viewed their employees as being unusually resistant to change. There's an old war story saying that anything that challenges an established routine automatically gets rejected. The managers can cite example after example of how people have obstructed their plans, refused to complete new tasks, and generally made their lives miserable.
>
> As a result, a discussion about how to inform employees of an imminent change is fraught with anxiety. Around the table, brows are furrowed and everyone keeps squirming in their seats. Team members talk about the need to sneak the change in under the radar; otherwise, they fear, the opposition will be too strong.
>
> Finally, somebody gets the idea to take a look at how the management has informed employees about previous new projects. Two individuals are assigned to investigate the matter.
>
> When they present their findings at the next meeting, it becomes clear that communications in the past have left a lot to be desired, and therefore the employees' reluctance is perfectly understandable. Gradually, the focus of the discussion shifts to a thoughtful, factually based examination of the information channels within the organization. In the end, the team decides to be much more proactive this time. While they will still stand by the change, they will do a better

CHAPTER 9

> job of explaining their rationale and give the employees more time to digest the new plans before putting them into place.
>
> Undoubtedly there will still be some protests. However, the process will be more open and straightforward than previous change initiatives, and that can have a positive effect in the long run.

Notice that the working group in this example is able to stay focused on the task at hand, while at the same time taking in more diverse and complex information, rather than complacently relying on habitual ways of thinking. We can see the quality of present-moment attentiveness both in their thinking and in their working climate.

Cultivating a basic attitude of listening and paying attention is well worth your while, particularly in your professional role. Whatever work you do, whatever function or position you have, it's important to be able to look reality in the eye.

Applying the model to your workplace

The following exercise is designed to help you use the model on page 88 as a basis for reflection, either individually or in a group.

EXERCISE

- Consider which time frame occupies most of your thinking. Do you often get drawn into memories? In social situations, do you spend much time wondering what other people are thinking? Are you very busy planning things for the future, big or small?
- Now focus on what happens just in your professional life. Start with the top row. Which square do you end up in most frequently, and what do you do there? Do you rehash old war stories from your current job or previous workplaces? Do you think back wistfully about how perfect things were at your old job? Do you spend a lot of time in meetings wondering what people are really thinking, but not saying? Do you tend

> to leave briefings about upcoming changes feeling anxious or fearful? Or do you find yourself hoping for miraculous solutions to complicated problems?
>
> - The bottom row is the place you need to be when you're working. In which work contexts are you able to do this type of thinking? When are you able to recognize that the past is multifaceted and the future is uncertain? When do you base your actions and decisions on facts and direct experiences, and not on hastily drawn conclusions from the past? How often do you stay fully present in the current moment and check in with your colleagues to make sure you've understood each other properly, instead of allowing nagging questions and uncertainties to remain unspoken?

By asking yourself these types of questions and using the model as a map of your mental processes, you can get a better understanding of the way you think about your work and what you might need to change. You can also look more broadly at your team or your workplace, and gain insight into the group's common patterns of thinking: Do people throughout your department frequently get caught up in war stories? Does your team look at all the relevant facts before making an important decision? And so on.

The model can also be used as a feedback tool after meetings. You can ask yourselves, "Which box did we spend the most time in? Was it functional? Have we been sufficiently focused and present?"

In the course of our daily life and work, our thinking moves back and forth between the boxes. Tracking these patterns can help improve our ability to notice when a train of thought is not useful—when it gets in the way of our work, prevents us from seeing things clearly, or makes our job more difficult or stressful. When our communication and thought patterns are on the top row, this is often a signal that we're at risk of dropping out of our role. By the same token, it is often easier to take up our role when we stay grounded on the bottom row.

CHAPTER 10

Hanging in for the long haul

The focus of this book has been on how we clarify and shape our roles at work. A common thread running through all the topics we've discussed is the need to shift from a self-focused, person-driven attitude to a task-oriented, performance-driven approach. Thoughtfully completing the exercises in each chapter, and revisiting them when necessary, can help you avoid the common pitfalls and roadblocks that make this a difficult task for many people. In this final chapter, we briefly summarize some of the key points we hope you'll take away from this book and offer a few concluding words of guidance.

Contextual factors that help us take up our role

- Clarity regarding the purpose, mission, and goal of what we're doing.
- Coherent description of the broader context, including sufficient information regarding how the organization as a whole is structured and how it functions.
- A clear description of what our professional role entails and what function we're expected to fulfill in our team or department.
- Effective transfer of information and clarity around the formal channels of communication.

- Orderliness in all meetings, including a shared understanding of each meeting's purpose, content, and agenda, and how the participants are expected to contribute.

What can we do ourselves?

- Realize that there's a difference between our overall personality and the various roles we take up.
- Develop and maintain a mental filter that separates our personal self from our professional role.
- Identify and use the skills and aspects of our personality that are functional in any particular role.
- Actively contribute to building a functional manager-employee relationship.
- Be aware that we form part of a group that goes through various developmental stages, and participate constructively in these stages.
- Remember the importance of focusing on the here and now, with a fact-seeking attitude, in both our thinking and our communication.
- Be careful to share information and discuss issues in the appropriate forums.

Don't reinvent the wheel

In most companies, a lot of work goes into describing the organization's operations and objectives, the roles of the employees, and the attitudes and behaviors that are desirable within that context. Unfortunately, this information often gets forgotten and is rarely applied in any practical way.

Many workplaces have a history of aborted change initiatives and development projects that never led anywhere—perhaps because the forums, documents, and structures that were already in place, and that the management and coworkers could recognize, were not used.

If you continue to work on the issues set out in this book within the context of your job, you'll probably be able to find a fair amount of relevant material in-house. This can save you a considerable amount of time. By reading through documents such as business plans, mission statements, and balanced scorecards, and finding out about the decisions made at planning sessions or corporate strategy meetings, you can learn about things that should have been done but have never been implemented. Typically, the resources and tools required for taking up your role and working effectively are already there; it's just a matter of using them. Performance reviews, department meetings, and strategic retreats are just a few examples of existing forums that can be used for this type of developmental work. The following exercise outlines two important steps you can take within the framework of these meetings.

EXERCISE

1. Go through the documents that govern the functioning of your organization, such as mission statements, balanced scorecards, and business plans. Consider how well or poorly they reflect the current reality at work. Do you understand what they mean? Is the wording abstract or sufficiently concrete, useful, and directive? In what ways can you use the documents so that they provide helpful guidance in your day-to-day work?

2. Pull out your employment contract and other documentation that applies to your role, and go through these materials with your manager. How are your role and your responsibilities described? Talk together about your reaction to those descriptions. Should the role be designed in the way that it's currently described? Or have the expectations changed? If so, in what way?

CHAPTER 10

We humans have a strong tendency to forget what we actually know—that it is only through ongoing, consistent effort that sustainable development takes place. Many of us find it easy to feel energized about starting a new process, but difficult to hang in there until the end. It takes patience to keep working at something for a long time.

Moreover, in any team or organizational development process, it's easy to get worried about being too confined and limited by structures and procedures. But paradoxically, the activities that truly help you to develop—such as clarifying professional roles, communication channels, and goals—often leave both employees and managers with a much greater sense of freedom and purpose. One of our colleagues illustrates this point with an analogy:

> **Imagine that you're on an eighth floor balcony without a railing. How do you feel? How are you likely to behave?**

Most people would feel rather tense and would hardly move at all around the balcony. Many of us would keep our backs pressed against the wall, staying as far away from the ledge as possible.

> **Now imagine that there's a solid, secure railing on that balcony. How do your feelings and behavior change?**

We would probably feel safer and dare to go all the way to the edge, maybe even leaning out over the edge to look at the view.

In the same way, having a clear framework for the work we do provides an enhanced sense of security and enables us to be more daring, exploring the full range of opportunities that are available to us. This makes it easier to leave behind our personal agendas and self-focused behavior, and increases our chances of being both efficient and effective. It is then that we can begin to find true satisfaction and fulfillment in our work.

REFERENCES

Agazarian, Y.M. (1997). *Systems-centered therapy for groups.* New York: Guilford Press.

Agazarian, Y.M. & Gantt, S.P. (2000). *Autobiography of a theory: Developing a theory of living human systems and its systems-centered practice.* London: Jessica Kingsley Publishers.

Antonovsky, A. (1991). *Hälsans mysterium.* Stockholm: Natur och Kultur.

Antonovsky, A. (1987). *Unraveling the Mystery of Health: How People Manage Stress and Stay Well.* San Francisco, CA: Jossey-Bass.

Gantt, S.P. & Agazarian, Y.M. (Eds.) (2006). *SCT in action: Applying the Systems-Centered Approach in Organizations.* London: Karnac Books.

Lundberg, P & Henrysson Eidvall, S (2010). *Träna ledarskap.* Stockholm: Liber.

Sandahl, C., Falkenstrom, E., & von Knorring, M. (2010). *Chef med kansla och fornuft—om professionalism och etik i ledarskapet.* Stockholm: Natur och Kultur.

Wheelan, S.A. (2005). *Group processes: A developmental perspective (2nd ed).* Boston: Pearson Education.

Wheelan, S.A. (2010). *Att skapa effektiva team: En handledning för ledare och medlemmar.* Lund, Sweden: Studentlitteratur.

Wheelan, S.A. (2009). Creating Effective Teams: *A Guide for Members and Leaders* (3rd ed). Thousand Oaks, CA: Sage.

www.systemscentered.com
www.gdqassoc.com
www.sandahls.se

ORDERING INFORMATION

Additional copies of *Taking Up Your Role* can be ordered online at http://catalystpress.bigcartel.com.

Alternatively, you can contact the publisher directly:

Ben Benjamin
Catalyst Communications Press
ben@catalystcommunicationpartners.com
t: 800.600.1522

Bulk orders (10 or more copies) receive a 20% discount.